DON'T SELL WE'RE BRITISH!

DON'T SELL
WE'RE BRITISH!

TONY DIMECH

bookshaker

First Published in Great Britain 2011
by www.BookShaker.com

© Copyright Tony Dimech

This book is dedicated to Susan, Hayley and Peter.

Life is what you make it, and you make mine special.

TONY DIMECH

Tony Dimech has spent more than twenty five years in a sales and business development environment. He currently heads up appleton associates, one of the UK's leading sales development companies. Established in 1998, it is one of the few sales training & consultancy practices whose focus is dedicated to 'Sales Training', 'Sales Coaching',

'Sales Process', and 'Sales Turnaround' offering a complete support package to organisations in pursuit of sales excellence. He is also a director of Motive9, which is a business development consultancy that specialises in the integration of business strategy and online strategy.

Tony's career has taken him through some of the country's leading branded suppliers to industry. Tony has been working within the area of personal development since 1985. During this time he has created a reputation of being a great motivator of people, instilling pride and passion into their everyday routines.

He has personally run sales training programmes in over twenty countries for some major blue chip companies. His training style focuses on getting delegates out of their comfort zones and motivated to use new techniques, becoming a catalyst to bring about a shift in the organisational DNA. He believes that effective learning has to be relevant, participative and FUN! Tony's courses have received rave reviews from both delegates and managers.

Tony's greatest strengths are his drive and passion for selling. He still enjoys the buzz of selling and thrives on a new challenge.

He lives in Buckinghamshire with his wife and family. When not working he enjoys music, photography, sailing and travelling.

CONTENTS

FOREWORD

I am honoured to be asked to write the foreword to this fabulous user friendly book on selling skills. I have known Tony Dimech for some years. The first encounter being 'on the job' as it were, developing selling skills in a member of staff who went on to become one of the most successful sales people I have known. My business development mind can put a strategic business plan together but without good people to deliver the sales targets required it all falls at the first fence. So I listened into Tony and learned a lot!

Tony has the innate ability to bring out the best in people around him. This intelligent, experienced and light hearted man is a great example of his chosen profession. He firstly sells himself to the uninitiated and then he sells them the skills they need. He has written this informative and amusing book to assist you, the reader, to develop your own sales skills and get the most out of a multitude of sales situations.

In this world of multi-cultural businesses and influences Tony never forgets he is dealing with people. It is my belief, that, in order to be a successful sales person, you need to have a liking for people. If not, before long it will show and the sales will simply not happen as readily as they should. Tony's warm personality makes it easy to feel comfortable around him. He uses many well proven techniques in his sales approach, for example his application of psychology to assist the overall sales goal. Sales environments need flexible, agile minds to engender the desired results. Every sales situation is different so it is the creative, well researched and highly prepared representative who will do well in this specialism.

In this book Tony tackles the thorny issue of Selling to Brits. Not the easiest group of punters to approach. We can be judgemental, objectionable and dismissive. Many cultures around the world are easier to sell to, often taking on face value the unique selling points of a product or service. Although we wouldn't like to admit it, we have a built in cultural response which is tough on sales people. Our natural pessimistic view of sales representatives can make us sceptical, distrustful and problematic to sell to. At the best of times we Brits are a sales challenge of considerable magnitude. What Tony dissects here is how to meet that challenge, break through the scepticism, establish belief and create that sale!

Of the readers who will take time to pour over the words of considerable wisdom within these pages, there will be amongst you a variety of sales situations, personalities and job specifications. Also everyone learns differently and at different speeds. So to each of you this book presents, an opportunity to learn at your own speed, in your own way and relate it to your own situation. The book prompts you to take action as you go along. There are road signs to show you the way forward and question marks to prompt your interaction with the text putting your own situational spin on the information. In this way you can personalise the learning experience to your current needs.

I can highly recommend this new professional sales book. This step by step guide to sales will ensure greater clarification of your sales purpose and timetabling of your goals. It will help you develop a structured framework and disciplined plan for your day and your week. Indirectly this guide should help you achieve a structured pathway to develop your own ultimate sales career. I sincerely hope you enjoy the book as much as I have done. More importantly I hope you use the information held within to successfully further your career in sales to your optimum potential.

Roisin Isaacs MBA

Shareholder and Company Director of Nationwide Healthcare Connections Ltd, Healthcare Connections Ltd and Healthcare on Call Group Ltd. Star of Channel 4's Secret Millionaire, May 10th 2009

PREFACE

It was a cold, wet and windy day in 1982 when I set out from Swansea to Staines for an interview. Whilst I felt quietly positive about the interview, there seemed to be forces telling me not to go. The day before my car had developed a problem so I had borrowed on from a good friend. I left in plenty of time as I somehow knew the journey would not be a straightforward one.

Dressed in my best suit with my highly polished shoes, new shirt and tie I set off five hours before the allotted time of two o' clock. I had not been in the car more than thirty minutes when the rain got much worse causing traffic to slow down almost to a halt. There were long delays at the Severn Bridge; I was pleased with myself for allowing so much time. As I passed the bridge I could see the sky getting even darker: this was not going to be a pleasant journey.

About ten minutes later everything suddenly went black: I realised the bonnet on David's car had popped up as I was doing fifty miles an hour on the M4! Not being able to see anything ahead was very scary. I indicated and slowly pulled left onto the hard shoulder and got out to have a look.

By the time I had got the bonnet down I was soaked wet through. What was I to do now? Carry on and get to the interview looking like a vagabond or give in to the forces and turn around. I decided to carry on and find somewhere to tidy up before going to the interview. The rest of the journey was carried out in the slow lane (not one I had ever used much prior to that day) travelling at speeds around 30 miles per hour, getting some very strange looks from everybody who passed me!

Eventually I arrived at Staines and found the offices; I drove past them to the nearest pub (no, not for a drink although I certainly needed one!) and found the quietest corner of the car park. Stripping all my wet clothes off and turning the heating up full blast I reckoned I had about ten minutes to dry them. After ten minutes I dressed again in the heavily steamed up car and headed to the pub toilets to straighten myself up, I looked at myself in the mirror and could not believe my eyes. None of the preparation was apparent and I looked a mess! Yet again I thought about turning back and heading home, but something inside told me not to.

Ten minutes later I was in the reception area waiting to meet the sales director. He ushered me into his office offered me a coffee and a cigarette (it was a long time ago), and asked, "Did you have a good journey down?" I accepted both and told him exactly what had happened. He took one look at me and said "If that is true, I certainly admire your tenacity." I suddenly realised that not turning round and going home was exactly the right decision.

Almost thirty years on I still look back and reminisce on that day. I still know that I made the right decision as that day changed my life: I was offered my first position in sales!

Tony Dimech

ACKNOWLEDGEMENTS

To the late Phillip Laycock (The sales director referred to on the previous page) my first sales mentor and role model.

To Richard Moksa for his development methods and his faith in me.

To Rory Cullinan for a truly inspirational work experience.

To Debs Jenkins for believing in this book and Joe Gregory for getting it to print.

To Paul Wright for his help with this project.

WHY SELLING TO THE BRITISH IS SO DIFFERENT

It has puzzled me for many years why the American image of sales-people is so very different to the UK and Europe. American sales-people are treated with respect, like friends, and certainly without the cynicism meted out to their European counterparts.

In business, American sales-people are regarded as professionals in the same way as accountants, bank managers and lawyers.

Why is this the case?

I believe one of the primary reasons is that, in America, most people *enjoy* being sold to! When they go out to buy something they *expect* to be sold to. For example, most of us can remember seeing something like this on American TV.

Man and wife walk onto used car lot called Big Sam's (or whatever) and look at a Chrysler V8 gas-guzzler.

Enter Big Sam who greets them with:

"Hiya folks. Welcome to Big Sam's used car emporium. Are we gonna do a deal today or are we gonna do a deal today?"

Man and wife smile warmly at Big Sam.

"Yeah, we are gonna do a deal today Big Sam."

Two hours later, man and wife have a new car. They know the names of all Big Sam's kids, they know where he lives and he is their newest best friend.

Could this conversation happen in the UK or Europe? I would suggest that it's very unlikely because, in the UK, we are culturally different. Our approach to many things is different and this includes our attitude to sales-people. Our overall mind-set towards selling (and, by extension, our overall attitude to buying) is different. In the UK people don't want to be sold to: they want sales-people to provide them with specific information then leave them to make the final decision for themselves. They are fine with buying, if only you could do it without the selling part.

If you have been in sales for any length of time I am sure you will have heard of a sales process called 'The ABC of Selling'. It is quite simple. It stands for Always Be Closing. Over the years it has become a well-known selling mantra. You may already know where it emanates from but, if you don't, I'm guessing by now that you know what's coming.

Yes, that's right: it's American.

It is a perfect fit for the American sales culture but it is not such a good fit for ours. Yet, despite our cultural differences, for the last fifty years the majority of sales training materials that are used in the UK and Europe have been sourced from the USA. I believe this is the dominant driver behind the negativity so many sales-people have to overcome. When you consider this in more detail it should come as no surprise to learn that most people in the UK dislike sales-people as most of them have been trained to sell in a manner that is inappropriate to our fundamental cultural requirements. So it is little wonder we have such a bad reputation!

The British are different!

British people (and in this I include people from anywhere in the world who consider their cultural origin to be British) respond to sales-people along a line that starts at caution and proceeds through suspicion to outright hostility. We want things; of course we do, and most of us have had to sell at some point in our lives; Britain is among the greatest trading nations on earth. But as individuals we value our privacy, and unashamed ABC selling is invasive.

Always Be Closing assaults our finer sensibilities. We are the modest virgins of the sales world, who must be wooed with a consultative approach. Being talked at by someone who is overtly aiming for a sale turns us well and truly off. We want to feel that we are in control, and that we are buying what we want, not what the seller wants to sell to us.

INTRODUCTION

I am British and I have chosen to make my living for the past thirty years in sales. I know, as you know, that ABC doesn't work as well as we need it to. What you don't know, although happily I do, is that there is another approach that does work. I've called it ABCD.

I learned by trial and error. In fact some may say I learned the hard way, but I disagree because I have loved every single moment of it. However, if you had asked me thirty years ago: "Tony, here is a short cut through some of the trials and errors. Would you like it?" I would probably have taken your arm off at the shoulder!

So, I decided to write this book to help professional sales-people like you and I to appreciate the subtle differences we have to make in our sales approach in order to succeed in the UK and other similar cultural environments. It isn't difficult - in fact in many respects it is easier, because what you will be doing is more natural and a better fit culturally.

So the first lesson you have to learn is this:

The role of a British sales-person isn't to 'sell' in the American sense. If you want to sell to British customers (and other customers who have somehow acquired the famous British reserve), you have to do something different.

You have to make your potential customers want to buy.

You have to create demand!

The 'ABC-D' of selling!

4

No, it doesn't stand for, Always Be Closing...Don't! My ABCD stands for... Always Be Creating Demand!

ALWAYS BE CREATING DEMAND

You can call it Desire, if you like. I often do. Either way we are talking about keeping the emphasis on creating a proposition that is shaped around what the customer wants. In our job we are contacting, networking, following up, and our aim is never to concentrate on the close: our challenge is to create demand for what we offer.

Everything we say and do should ensure we increase the amount of desire the customer has to do business with us, so much so I believe we can safely say, "It is not our job to SELL, it is our job to make customers want to buy from us!" Call it facilitating the buying process if you like.

Once that's done, closing is the easiest part of the job. In fact, if you create enough demand, you don't ever need to close. The client or customer doesn't need to be "closed on". Like an expertly created meal, when it's done, it's done. No further work required.

So, how do we create demand?

Well to start with, we have to put our customers, potential and existing, FIRST!

Yeah, I know. Radical eh?

We find out:

- Exactly what they are trying to do and what challenges they face

- What will help them to achieve their goals
- What their customers are demanding of them
- How we can potentially help them achieve their goals
- What doubts they may have about committing to the transaction
- Why it's in their interests to deal with us, not our competitors
- In fact we have to find out as much as we can about any sales opportunity

The key to achieving this is *differentiation*. We have to differentiate ourselves from our competitors by gaining a better appreciation of the customer's precise requirements; if we do this well we can shape our proposition to fit their expectations. By doing this better than our competitors we will offer a more compelling proposition and we will create more demand. The more demand we create for the proposition the more we make the customer want what we can provide rather than what our competitors offer.

If you can master the art of creating desire or demand, closing the sale is not difficult.

And if you want a route map for how to create demand to buy, how about another mnemonic list:

- **A**ttitude
- **B**ackground research
- **C**uriosity (questioning skills)
- **D**efence against objections.

Over the coming chapters, we will discover what each of these really mean but just to whet your appetite consider this: without genuine curiosity and innovative questioning skills, you can't build background. Without background, you can't create demand. Until you create demand you have not created any differentiation. Without differentiation, you face an uphill struggle to overcome objections, which will have a negative impact on your attitude. Without attitude, you will lose heart before you master your ABCD... and so it goes on.

This is why you should consider following my ABCD. If you do I promise you the road to successful selling will be a lot less challenging and a lot more enjoyable, not to mention rewarding!

So let's look more closely at how you can Always Be Creating Demand.

THE SALES JOURNEY

There is a way we thread our skills together to reach our goal. It is the process of selling. Underlying it is a structure. It's like a journey in a storybook where the hero sets out armed with a sword to persuade the Great King to let him marry his daughter. The snag? The great king doesn't know our hero from Adam, and the daughter is already flirting with another prince.

As sales-people we undertake the hero's journey hundreds, some of us thousands, of times a year. If we're any good, we begin with the end in mind, just as the Hero does. Our aim is to get the Great King to allow his daughter to marry us instead of the other princes who may have shinier swords, rounder shields or bigger jousting tents. We want him to want what we offer, and want it from us, not a competitor.

Inevitably we will make false starts, but I have learned during many years of selling that *Attitude*, *Background* research, *Curiosity* (created and managed throughout by exceptional questioning) and a full armoury of *Defences* work a lot better than *Always Be Closing* ever did.

On the journey we will certainly meet dragons (usually on the switchboard or in reception) and face the Supreme Ordeal (the toughest objection you ever heard). So we make sure we are prepared, and carry defences that we wield like the hero's sword. And we practise, so that we become true warriors who never shirk at the prospect of another tough battle.

If you think this is just whimsy, ask yourself this question: "Is it possible that I may be stuck in a paradigm?"

Paradigms can seriously harm your wealth. Just ask the guy who turned down the Beatles because "there was no more call for another guitar band" or the investor who said "Mobile telephones are a gimmick. They will never catch on!" And how many publishers thought JK Rowling's Harry Potter was never going to be a success?

Attitude, *Background*, *Curiosity* and *Defences* provide a structure to the task to *Always Be Creating Demand*.

Master your armoury of *Attitude*, *Background*, *Curiosity* and *Defences*, and you will reduce the number of false trails you pursue, increase your sales and you know what?

You will enjoy your job a lot more, you will become more successful, and you will start to earn a lot more money.

This book is therefore structured around these four key skills. At every stage *creating demand* is the underpinning theme. When we talk about attitude we are aiming at creating an *Attitude that Creates Demand*. And it's the same for all the other sections.

One other thing you should know before we get started: I am going to ask you to work while you read. Throughout the book I will ask you questions and invite you to write down your answers. I have done this because I want you to find out what this all means for you. I already know what it means for me but I am not you, and your experiences and situations are different to mine, so the way you interpret what I suggest and how you go on to make sense of it will be unique to you. By completing the exercises you will gain a better comprehension of what this book is about. I will be your guide but you are the one on the journey.

 So when you see this symbol, you know it's time to get your pad and pen out. In fact do that right now and think about what you believe selling really is. Try to capture your definition in one sentence.

Turn the page when you are done, and compare your definition with mine.

Selling is:

> *"Selling is the art of letting other*
> *people have your own way!"*
> **TONY DIMECH**

I believe selling is an art. It certainly isn't a science, and I believe that, if you are in the right frame of mind, ask the right questions, listen carefully to the answers, and use the information you gather to shape the proposition to fit the true requirements of your customer, *your* way will create sufficient demand to make that customer want to do business with you!

FRAME OF MIND **A**	**UNDERSTANDING & APPLICATION OF SALES PROCESS** **B**
D **HANDLING OBJECTIONS**	**C** **QUESTIONING SKILLS**

I hope by now I have created sufficient demand for you to turn over to the next page, and get you started on the ABCD journey to more a satisfying sales career, conducting more business transactions together with customers who treat you with a lot more respect.

INTRODUCTION

CHAPTER ONE

ATTITUDE

If you're not in the right frame of mind to do business how can you expect your customers to be?

Do you remember this old cliché?

'Whether you believe you can or whether you believe you can't, you're absolutely right.'

Your attitude is fundamentally linked to what you believe to be true. Here is a typical belief that I have heard from professional sales-people:

"I believe that all buyers are at best devious; at worst dishonest wheeler-dealers who want to screw me down in every possible way."

Perhaps this is a belief you share.

 Imagine for a moment what attitude this belief creates. Get yourself a sheet of paper and write down as many attitudes (and emotions) that you can think of that would show what a person with this belief would be thinking. If you could slice open their attitude what would you see?

Turn the page when you are done.

My guess is you have written down some (but hopefully not all) of these:

- defensive
- aggressive
- distrustful
- timid
- challenging
- bored
- disrespectful
- prepared to do battle
- submissive
- hesitant

- focussed on 'winning'
- hopeful
- smug
- removed
- determined
- a feeling of 'here we go again'
- tired
- cold
- standoffish

Now circle all the words on your list (or ones on my list if you'd prefer) that will unquestionably help you to create demand.

When I did this I thought that the only two that might be helpful were 'challenging' and 'determined' although I had some reservations about both of them and asked myself:

"If I held this belief, what would I be challenging? And what would I be determined to do?"

What do you think?

Looking at it like this I decided that actually, none of them would help me to create demand. So, my belief has created a set of attitudes and emotions that will do nothing to help me create demand.

I believe that, if you think this way, you cannot create demand. The only plus side to this belief is at least you have thought about it and recognised its ability to drive your attitude.

And there may be additional impacts of the 'wrong attitude': not enough leads, not enough new business, an inability to recognise exciting new potential business, complacency with existing accounts ...

However, there are other beliefs that will drive a different kind of attitude. Suppose you believed this:

"All buyers are professional people who are trying to do their best for their business in very difficult conditions."

 Like we did earlier, imagine for a moment what attitude this belief creates. Write down as many attitudes (and emotions) that you can think of that would show what a person with this belief would be thinking. If you could slice open their attitude what would you see?

Turn the page when you are done.

Here is what I thought:

- sociable
- empathetic
- positive
- determined
- helpful
- curious
- sympathetic
- keen to help
- supportive
- concerned
- optimistic

- gentle
- empowered
- challenging
- recognising each customer's unique circumstances
- respectful
- accepting
- focussed on helping

Now, circle all the words that would help you to create demand.

An outsider looking in through a window would probably see the same behaviour from the buyers in both cases. The sales-person's attitude to the buyers however will be completely different. In the case of the second belief it's a lot easier to start to think about how you can create demand. And this is why it is so important to think about and manage your attitude.

If you were to do this, you will already be doing something that very, very few sales-people ever do and that puts you in the top 10% before you have even reached chapter two!

In real life, you will probably find that you have some beliefs that fall in between these two. So just spend a couple of minutes thinking about your own beliefs.

What do you believe about the buyers you work with? What attitudes do these beliefs create? Which of these will help you to create desire?

Another interesting thing about beliefs is: the more you look for evidence to support them, the more evidence you will find. For example, spend a day with the first of the two beliefs above and see what evidence you can find to support it. Then do the same thing with the second belief. My guess is you will find evidence to support both depending on which belief you are working with. This leaves you with a choice. Decide which belief you choose to accept, understanding that whichever one you choose will be true and will drive your attitude.

I have worked with many sales-people who go to visit customers and have given no thought to their frame of mind. Personally I think this oversight is unforgivable. The most valuable asset any sales-person has is their potential sales revenue (often referred to as the sales funnel): not to maximise the amount of sales revenue you harvest from your sales funnel inexcusable. Not being in the best possible frame of mind will do one thing: reduce the likelihood of you achieving your objectives for that sales call (if indeed you bothered to set any).

Being in the right frame of mind can have a huge impact on the outcome of any sales call. I would bet money that anyone reading this book has experienced both sides of the coin here. You must have made at least one call when you were in such a positive frame of mind you were unstoppable! And at least one sales call where you were so negative you never had a chance. Well your next lesson is to learn how to get yourself in that frame of mind where you feel unstoppable for every call. I want you to think about this for a moment: just imagine that with a little bit of effort you will be able to visit any customer in a frame of mind that will give you a huge competitive edge. What impact would this have on your life?

 This is such an important part of the journey that I want you to list some of the advantages you would experience if you were able to take control of your attitude before going in to ALL of your sales calls.

If that doesn't convince you that this is worth the effort then stop reading now!

If it has, come with me and I will take you to a very special place, called...

'THE ZENITH ZONE'

Getting into the *Zenith Zone*. The mood indicator.

What's your mood this minute? Unstoppable, reasonable, bad, or downright awful? The first step to getting into a positive frame of mind is to honestly position how you feel at a precise moment in time. I cannot emphasise enough the importance of honesty here. Don't trick yourself that you are feeling positive when you are not: you will only be lying to yourself. And if you are prepared to lie to yourself, to what lengths will you go to deceive your customers (and some of us thought buyers were dishonest and deceitful!). To help you do this I have included my version of a very simple 'Mood Meter'. This can be used at any time (five minutes before you make a sales call is a great time to establish how you are feeling).

 Honestly align your feelings at this precise moment with one of the scales of the mood meter on the next page.

THE MOOD METER

I'm amazing. In fact I'm too good for this job.	**10**
Fantastic. I am in total control of my feelings, I am prepared for every eventuality in the next call and nothing can stop me achieving my call objectives!	**9**
Every day's an adventure. My home life and work life are well balanced. I occasionally get a bit down but I know how to control it.	**8**
I know how to do my job although I sometimes don't do it and I am always on the lookout for ways to make life more exciting and interesting.	**7**
I know when things are not going so well but it's too hard to change so I wait for it to pass.	**6**
I have my good days and my bad days. I never really think about why that is.	**5**
I get up and I do the job. It pays for my interests outside work. That's my life and I quite like it like this.	**4**
I guess I could do more with my life but it's hard to get motivated.	**3**
I get up, I do the job, I go to bed. That's my life. It's quite boring but what can I do?	**2**
I hate my job, my life, everything is so difficult. Why on earth did I bother getting out of bed this morning?	**1**

THE ZENITH ZONE

So where do you think the *Zenith Zone* is positioned on the mood meter?

Without doubt '9' is the place to be! It's the height of the *Zenith Zone*. A sales-person at '10' is too impulsive; they will talk too fast and won't stop telling their customer how good their offer is; they will talk at customers without listening to what they want (you will learn later that 'Telling isn't Selling'); they will not create demand!

'7' or below isn't good enough.

You can't sell when you let the everyday annoyances of life get to you. Why? Because you are not in your *Zenith Zone*. If you were arguing before you left home or were the victim (or culprit) of 'Road Rage' on the way to work, you'll approach your job in a negative mood. You won't care enough; you won't be confident enough; you won't be focussed on your primary and secondary call objectives. You won't be asking questions that enable your customer to realise how different you are from your competitors. Instead you'll babble on without listening to what your customers are really saying, and you won't spot sales opportunities. You'll make a lasting impression on your customers, which will not be a positive one!

Everybody has days like this and some people can afford them less than others. Sales-people can't afford them at all! As a sales-person, you need to devise your own strategies that will get you into your *Zenith Zone* whenever you want.

I firmly believe that a major differentiator between mediocre sales-people and super sales-people is their ability to get into their *Zenith Zone* whenever they need to.

Just take some time out for a moment and imagine what your life would be like if you perfected this. I can imagine the smile on your face as I write this, knowing you had the internal power to become 'Unstoppable' whenever you needed to. How would that impact upon your ability to realise your goals and expectations? There is no end to what you could achieve if you perfected this routine.

Please don't think it is easy – it isn't! However it is simple and it is possible, and certainly worth the effort it takes to develop.

Don't believe you can? Try this.

 Sit like you would if you were completely bored. Remember a time when you were completely bored. Notice how realistic the feeling of boredom is. Are you bored? Well my guess is you are starting to feel bored. If someone were to ask you right now what your attitude was, you may well reply:

"Yes, I do feel bored."

If you did this exercise, something strange may have happened to you and, if it did, I caused it. At the start of this exercise, your attitude initially was 'curiosity'. I changed your attitude from being curious to being bored. How? Simply by altering your frame of mind.

Am I clever? No, not really. This is a simple technique that I will teach you to do for yourself.

So take five minutes, have a walk about, shake off the feeling of boredom and come back feeling curious about how and why this works so well and why managing your attitude is a fundamental skill in *Always Be Creating Demand*.

See you in five minutes …

…Welcome back. OK let's explore the fundamental methodology behind the *Zenith Zone* principle.

GETTING INTO THE ZENITH ZONE

What you are about to read is possibly your first step towards a more positive existence. A life enriched with positivity because *you* chose to abandon negativity. Here is my method to elevate yourself into a better frame of mind with which to approach life and most certainly the right frame of mind for creating demand!

First of all take the mood indicator test. Remember to be honest with yourself. If you are down there at a '2' admit it. Some people think it is a sin to be feeling so low. That's ridiculous; the sin is to do nothing about it and continue making sales calls.

So if you are up there at '9' and in your *Zenith Zone,* fantastic: get out there and get selling! You know you are going to have a great day.

However if you are not, these next steps will prove to be invaluable. In a moment I am going to ask you to you put this book down for two minutes and capture your thoughts and feelings, but before you do read the instructions below fully.

 Shut your eyes and start to think about one of the happiest moments in your life. Think about the great times you have enjoyed in your professional or personal life. Think about your greatest achievements, the effort you put in to them. The elation you felt when you reached your goal. Think about how you felt when you sat back and reflected on your performance, and how great it felt to talk about it. Think of the things that make life so wonderful for YOU! – Things you have done, things you are planning to do. Music you have listened to, books you have read, films that had a lasting impact on you, just think of anything that has inspired you or made you feel '*on top of the world*'. See what you saw, hear what you heard, feel what you felt when you felt on top of the world.

Then open your eyes, and in your notebook write down a list of those things that make you feel terrific.

OK, your two minutes start NOW!

At this point people can think of a myriad different things, each one having a special place in their soul. Some people think about the love of their families, others think of the energy of their friends, fantastic holidays they've had or are going to have, the marathon they'll soon run, or some other event they are training hard for. They think about their football team winning a major trophy, or the time they drove down to France with their friends, or the impromptu nights out they enjoyed at the drop of a hat and with no planning.

For you it may be one or more of those things; or it may just be waking up to the smile on your children's faces or the fragrance of the roses on a sunny day.

Whatever is in your mind *capture it*! Make your list. It doesn't matter how large or small the list is; it is the essence of the power you have within you to transform your life!

You see, this is the key: we can choose our attitude, we can accept we are not having the best time right now and feel sorry for ourselves, and as a result we can waste a lot of time, effort (albeit half hearted), and most importantly a lot of potential sales! Or we can chose to say that whatever the world may throw at us we can approach life in a positive frame of mind. Life may deal you some bad cards from time to time; however it's up to you how you play your hand! We all know that selling can instigate a variety of mixed emotions. Yet some of us forget it is one of the most rewarding professions, and it is our chosen arena. It is where we are expected to demonstrate our desire and ability to succeed.

How do you feel now?

I am certain you don't feel negative. I am also confident that you've gone up a point or two on the Mood Meter. Who knows, you may even be in the *Zenith Zone*.

I would like you to reflect on this session and ask yourself: "What have I learned?"

I hope you have begun to appreciate the power of a positive mental attitude. I hope you have learned that it is possible to take better control of your mental state at any time. I hope you have learned that just thinking about the things that make you feel terrific can take you to your *Zenith Zone*.

What have *you* learned from this session?

Capturing your thoughts and feelings will have another huge benefit. The brain is an amazing thing. It stores things in different ways depending on what you do. Writing things down transfers ideas and thoughts into the subconscious where it helps to build beliefs. By writing down all the great things in your life you enhance the effect these have on your attitude.

Oh, and by the way, have you ever been just about to go to sleep and a great idea comes to you and you think: I must remember this in the morning? And can you remember it in the morning? No, I can't either but I have learnt to keep a pad next to the bed. Just by writing the idea down helps me to recall it in the morning. I remember the idea before I have even opened my eyes to read the pad. I've even tried lying in bed writing in the air without a pad or a pen! It still works (although it took me a while to convince my wife that I was still sane). Try it. It's great.

You will notice a huge improvement in your sales results, your energy levels and your overall happiness if you learn how to get into your *Zenith Zone* and stay there for sustained periods. People will probably notice how positive you're looking, how upbeat you are about everything, and remember: positivity is infectious.

So how are you going to keep on doing this?

ZENITH ZONE ROUTINES

As you have experienced the effect of being in the *Zenith Zone* we are going to look at devising a simple routine that you can use anywhere to help bring about a positive change in your mental state and get you nearer that '9' on the mood indicator.

This is called creating "Anchors" and your life is stacked full of anchors that you have already created by accident. All I want you to do is to create some on purpose. Anchors can take many forms. For example, can you recall hearing a particular piece of music that maybe you haven't heard for ages, but as soon as it starts you are immediately transported back to the time when you first heard it, and all the emotions of that moment come flooding back? (This may be why we have 'Our Tunes')

Or maybe it's a particular smell? (I often have a bunch of fresh Freesias in my office. The smell reminds me of time when I was making a presentation to a very important potential customer, and there was a bunch on the table next to me. It went very well, I felt unstoppable, and guess what? Yes, I won the business. Now whenever I want to bring that feeling back all I have to do is smell Freesias.)

So what anchors do you already have? What are the sights or smells or sounds that create strong emotions in you? Or maybe it's something tangible; particular items of clothing perhaps that you know, when you wear them, you will have a good day? In fact, have you got something that you keep especially for when you want to feel good? (What do you think; cause or effect?)

To be able to jump right into your *Zenith Zone* whenever you want, you need to be aware of the anchors that will get you there fast. So try this:

Make more of a conscious effort to capture precious moments in your life and attach them to an anchor. If it's music, make yourself a compilation CD or a play list on your MP3 player, most of you will have the capability to put it on your phone, it is so easy these days to have this at your disposal 24-7. If it is not music but other precious items, keep them together in a box file or something similar. Try to take mementos from the great times you have in your life. It doesn't matter where you are, or what you are doing: if you are having fun think of a way to rekindle that feeling.

I have made a conscious effort to keep such things in a file so that I know I can always lift myself whenever the need arises. You can keep pictures, music, letters, postcards, concert tickets, boarding cards, commission slips; it doesn't matter what it is as long as the memories make you feel good. Then every month you can change some of them so that you never tire of the same routine, and so that you've always got a fresh stock of positive mental catalysts to motivate you.

Take two minutes to lift your mood whenever it flags, and your work (and life) will change for the better. On the telephone, you will be more positive than anyone else and you will sell more. You'll turn up for meetings in the right frame of mind: positive and enquiring, keen to listen and identify what you can do for the customer.

Are you going to win more business? What do you think?

Start now; start making the collection, in a folder or on your computer, of good things. Being in the *Zenith Zone* is basic to your success. In the *Zone*, you're in the right frame of mind to listen and observe carefully and ask the right questions that will reveal opportunities for selling.

You'll be proud of your job, proud of your company, proud to sell their products/services, and proud of their price. This will show itself in the way you stand; the way you look people in the eye, and most of all the way you speak. So when you come in to work grinning because you watched a DVD of *The Office* while you were gulping your coffee this morning, or because you listened to a song that makes you happy when you were driving in through the rain …

… and one of your less than motivated colleagues says,

"Here we go then, another bloody day in the workhouse!" You will resist the impulse to frown and get sucked into the negativity. You will leave the room and get out your little folder of fun (you smirking yet?) get yourself back into your *Zenith Zone* and be glad to be alive, and able to earn a great living.

STAYING IN YOUR ZENITH ZONE

Whatever your profession or sport, the high achievers rely absolutely on being able to get into the *Zenith Zone*. One percent of the world's population can run faster or further than the other ninety-nine percent of us, so there are a lot of good runners. So what puts world champions such as Kelly Holmes and Paula Radcliffe at the very top? It's not just that they have outstanding speed and stamina, which of course they do, but because they have consciously developed, like an extra muscle, their ability to override pain and anxiety every day of their lives. It's been said a thousand times: races are won in the head. You don't win gold medals without pounding the streets, the beaches, the track, thousands and thousands of times, against driving wind, across sand dunes, after a twenty-hour flight, in thirty-degree heat, in a rainstorm; all the times when the rest of us would indulge our aching knees, or let arguments get to us, or everyday worries. Achievers like Kelly and Paula have trained themselves to get into their *Zenith Zone* for the purpose of their work, and stay there.

Except – yes, you're right. Paula Radcliffe lost control just once, and you remembered, didn't you? The black mark hasn't faded yet. A world-class gold medallist in a sport most people would never even attempt, she still gets derisive comments from that single moment at the Athens Olympics when she fell by the wayside. Has she let it get to her? No. She has gone on to break records and win races because she can get into her *Zenith Zone* at will; and now she knows that not doing so is out of the question.

Sports psychologists call it a peak state. Actors and comedians must get into it. Perhaps they have spent the day with their sick child in hospital, but anxiety has to be wiped from the mood meter for six hours each evening, because the show must go on. They have to get into the *Zenith Zone* in order to go on stage and make people laugh – or, still harder, make them cry - while remaining in control of their own emotions.

Don't underestimate the difficulty of what you're doing. Comparison with professional acting and athletics is not an overstatement. Selling is a challenging profession, we all accept that. However, selling is your chosen arena, and while you are doing your job you must perform in your *Zenith Zone*. Not doing so is out of the question.

It is potentially damaging to ourselves and the company we represent. Let me be harsh here: you have to have a number of skills and characteristics to succeed in sales; if you don't have them you should be doing another job!

One of the most critical competencies required by salespeople is the ability to get themselves into their *Zenith Zone* whenever they need to; you will not achieve your goals and aspirations anywhere else! Despite its importance this aspect of sales performance is often overlooked and has become a major contributory factor as to why sales-people are behind target.

PERFECTING YOUR ZENITH ZONE ROUTINES

I must stress at this point that, whilst I totally believe in the methods I have divulged in this chapter, no routine will last forever. I liken this to music; quite often you will hear a piece of music that you find highly motivational. However if over the coming month that piece of music is overplayed it can cease to have the same effect; in fact if it is continually overplayed you can actually go off it. That very same song that used to elevate you immediately now has the opposite effect.

Well *Zenith Zone* routines are no different; one routine will never last forever, so vary yours. I find that by keeping my motivational items together in one place, it is easy to go through the collection every six to eight weeks, and alternate the items I keep to hand thereby updating my routine. Not only do I look forward to doing this, the contents always have the desired effect. Another benefit of this routine is that you tend to find the positive out of more situations because you look at them from a more constructive viewpoint. During the cold winter months you can be looking forward to the extra holiday in the sun you have booked thanks to the additional commission you earned. Another great positive technique for the winter months is to go out dressed in clothes that make you feel snug and comfortable despite the conditions there is a distinct sense of satisfaction when you can dress correctly and go out and beat nature!

According to Billy Connelly, "There is no such thing as bad weather, just the wrong clothes."

We could adapt this to selling and say, "There is no such thing as a bad customer, just a sales-person with the wrong attitude."

In sales you will encounter similar mental obstacles to overcome: the weather, the traffic, the difficult situation, and let's not forget the dreaded *cold call*. If there was one element of selling that most sales-people could eliminate from their job description it would be cold calling. However for most sales roles it is an integral function. We will cover this in chapter three, so for now let's stay in this very special place and enjoy our stay at the *Zenith Zone.*

AVOID NEGATIVITY & LOSE FALSE FRIENDS

Yes, that's right. Because negativity is more contagious than positivity and certain people are bad for you.

Have you any experience of competitive negativity? I have, I've seen it a thousand times. There are some people in every company who haven't got the clout or the courage to change anything but know exactly what is wrong with everything in it, from the locks on the toilet doors to the MD's relationship with the Finance Director. They are particularly aggrieved about the treatment they, personally, are getting. How can anybody expect them to do the job when the pay's crap, and the hours unreasonable, and there's no supervision, and did you hear what she said to that new guy in Media Sales, and so on, and so on, until you're ready to top yourself and it's still only nine-fifteen in the morning.

It's a competition to see who has the most negative story to tell at lunch time, when we are supposed to be re-charging ourselves ready for the challenges the afternoon will bring!

DON'T spend your valuable spare time with people like this, or you will rapidly become one!

I was once in the bar of a hotel at the end of the day when a guy bounced in, beaming, and strode up to his friend at the counter who was hunched over a drink. The friend looked at him.

"Looks like *you* had a good day."

"I had a GREAT day! I got it! I got that order." The salesman punched the air.

I'd been looking at the newcomer and thinking: he's getting it right. There's a guy with the attitude I like to see. That's the sort of person I want working for me.

His friend responded "All right for some, my day was awful…"

"Why? What happened?"

I could see the focus moving from the positive result to the negative experience

Five minutes later, on my way out to the foyer, I happened to walk past the two from the bar. They were both at a table now.

"And to top it all, do you know what he said to me? …" the miserable one was droning on.

The positive salesman looked deflated. He was listening to some sorry tale of failure and resentment. His body was slumped in the chair. His face was a mask of concern. All of his positivity had disappeared.

"What a waste!" I thought.

Your job is to show, and transmit, genuine enthusiasm. So you have to make it clear to anyone who breathes gloom into the air around you that you can't afford to catch negativity. It'll affect your income like a bad bout of 'flu.

If you catch negativity from anyone and end up colourless and glum, how can you expect your clients to be enthusiastic? On the phone they know from your tone of voice whether they can relate to you or not. They will forget ninety-three percent of what they hear and of the seven percent they retain, the impression you make is the biggest part: the way you made them feel.

Face to face, it's body language. Haul yourself out of your car with a sigh, lean back with folded arms while you listen to your customer's queries or slouch in your chair while you make a call, and you won't get the sale.

What if you, personally, feel deep-down negative about the whole business of selling?

If sales-people can't sell, it's usually because they're only in it for the money. They are unconvincing because they're not, personally, convinced. And if they think their customers are mugs, how persuasive are they going to be? Find a product you like or get excited about your luck at being able to earn so much money. Failing that, get a different job, because if you keep on doing the same old thing, you'll be very lucky to get the same old results.

If you are feeling low then decide in one word why, what is it that worries you today? Is there anything you can do about it in the next eight hours? If so, either take an hour out to make your move, or forget it; you have a living to earn. You are a salesman. You have to put your worries aside.

Just checking.

A great sales-woman that I know won't even listen to the radio in the mornings. She knows better than to drive in to work with a head full of war, robbery and plummeting house prices. She makes a point of listening to music she likes. Other such people play comedy radio programmes, or an uplifting piece of music, or even listen to a motivational speaker.

Part of the job in sales is managing the highs and lows, therefore your attitude is what counts. This has to be controllable. It's not simply a question of positive thinking. I've seen cold-callers take a deep breath and psych themselves up to lift the receiver off the phone:

"This is going to be the call where the patron saint of sales☞ smiles on me."

No, it isn't. This is hope taking over again, and if you rely on it you are setting yourself up for a long series of small, morale-sapping disappointments. You can get much the same effect from buying lottery tickets. The disappointments will be less frequent but just as inevitable.

Positive thinking can be a crutch. Any crutch has one obvious disadvantage: as soon as it's knocked away, you're flat on the floor. Instead you need to be in a calm, constructive and positive frame of mind because you know that your mood is within your control and, since it is essentially positive, you will make a good impression. If there are sales to be made, you'll make them.

THE ZENITH ZONE

If you have followed this chapter and completed the exercises you will have learned how to measure your current state of mind at any given moment and more importantly you will have ascertained how to improve your frame of mind whenever you need to! This could be the most powerful sales lesson you have ever learned! *Why*? Well you will never again be able to blame anyone or anything else for your negativity. The only person that has absolute power over your frame of mind is *you*! Yes others can influence it but you are the one that holds the

---

☞Saint Lucy of Syracuse, since you ask.

key and if you choose to hold on to that key you can unlock your positivity whenever you want to.

To complete this chapter I would like you to carry out one more task.

 I want you to visualise the future. I want you to imagine your future. I want you to believe that you will be in the right frame of mind for *every* call from this moment on. It is a fundamental ritual that you adhere to at all times. Now close your eyes and imagine the impact this new paradigm will have on your life. Think about the rewards, think about the additional satisfaction you will get from your job, think about the increased levels of success that you will enjoy simply by getting into your *Zenith Zone*. Think about these areas and any other area of your life that will be improved because of your power to control your frame of mind. Then capture your thoughts.

You know this is going to work… I can see you grinning from here!

CHAPTER TWO

PREPARATION

LOVING WHAT YOU DO – NOT DOING WHAT YOU LOVE!

I heard Maxie Jazz in a radio interview, being asked about his move to Britain from the Caribbean and the difficulties that presented. The interviewer started saying what a disappointment it must have been living here after Jamaica, considering the difference in the weather. Maxie said,

"Whoa. Stop. I came over knowing I was going to stay here. I knew the weather was different from Jamaica. In my head I just ran a program that made me adjust. I made myself like the cold and rainy weather, now I love the rain, I love the cold. Living here would have been unbearable if I didn't. I felt living here was just part of the big picture, I had to do it to get to my musical destination, so I thought Hey I'm going to enjoy it"

That is a winner's attitude!

STRETCH YOURSELF

If you can constantly stretch yourself, and you own expectations, you will reduce the risk of falling foul of one of the major sales temptations, to shape the job around your 'Comfort Zone'. I mean, come on! Who hasn't looked at the job and convinced themselves that they need to do more of what they are good at (what they like to do) and less of what they are not so good at (what they don't like to do).

Good sales-people devote time to learning where their clients' businesses stand in the market. It's about empathy: we all want to deal with people who can see our business from our point of view. And sales-people are in competition with each other.

Joe seems intent on selling me something.

Josephine wants to understand what my company is doing, why we're doing it and what we're aiming for.

Which of them is going to get my business?

Selling without consideration for what customers want or respect for what they've achieved is like saying 'You can have any colour as long as it's black.' Henry Ford could sell Model-Ts like that in the 1920s, but today's customers have a whole range of choices. Outrageous as it may seem, we all like to be treated like valued customers, or key customers, or even major customers when we're barely prospects yet. So while we're not exactly grovelling for tips like a hotel doorman, we have to file and recall, metaphorically, whether they like their shoes shined overnight and a chocolate on the pillow.

All preparation time pays off.

Target a customer and write down what you know about them.

Any gaps in your understanding? Thought so. If yours will be a business-to-business call, scan their website. Which market sector are they in? Who are they likely to be buying from? Have they changed any key personnel lately? Produced any radical new products? Where are they positioned within their industry? Who are their competitors and what are their competitors up to?

Your business is to create demand, so ration your time. Yes you need to spend some time researching your customers, but find your own most time-efficient route to the information you can need. Scan the online trade papers for their industry. Or check for archived news in the databases of the FT, business periodicals and broadsheet papers. Some of what's there may be completely irrelevant to them, but it will give you something to base your questioning strategy on when you are with them. 'I read that Blogg and Buggins are test marketing a supercharged version. Is that going to affect your business?'

Your first task is to get an appointment to see them, so if their website is not informative, don't be shy about asking them to drop you a brochure before your first meeting.

When you have made telephone contact and have an appointment to visit them, bear in mind which of your products is generally appropriate for a company of their size. Something you sell to SMEs may not be right for a multinational. Talk about this with people in other departments if you need to. Has the company you're with ever done business with them? If so, get the previous account records together. Is what happened last time relevant to what you're offering now? Are you approaching the same department? Have circumstances changed for them or for you? And is there anything about your offer that you could adapt to fit what they're likely to need?

It's a big mistake to build up fixed expectations before you meet a new client: they may, after all, not know what they want. Or they may be relieved to meet someone who'll offer them something they didn't know they could get. So don't fixate on any one thing you find out in the course of research. But equally, don't insult them by arriving with no idea of their business.

PUT YOURSELF IN THE BUYER'S SHOES

With a good attitude you'll want to understand the background of the people you're selling to. Variety and an opportunity to learn are, after all, what make selling interesting. However, some people just don't get it, and this was illustrated in a radio phone-in I heard recently.

The prolific writer and broadcaster Dr Raj Persaud had just launched a motivational book, and was taking calls at around two o'clock one afternoon. One of these calls was from a salesman parked in a lay-by in the rain. He was demotivated, stuck in a rut, parked in a metaphorical lay-by in his life and career as well in reality. His job was to sell water. There was water, water everywhere, teeming down the windscreen, splashing into puddles, bouncing off the roof. How, he wanted to know, could he motivate himself to sell water in a downpour?

This sad man, who said he was in it for the money, was acting as though water is just clear colourless wet stuff. Which was totally correct when in his shoes. However, to his clients, this isn't the case. To them, pure ice-cold drinking water on demand is central to production. If the drinking water runs out, the pace and value of work plummets, because the one thing we all need to operate at optimum capacity is a properly hydrated brain and body. And as social animals, we need a water-cooler as a focus in an office or a factory.

Was this guy even thinking about what his customer would value about his service? Was he thinking about which of them would need to increase their orders because they proposed to expand their factory's floor space? Or where he might suggest situating coolers in their retail outlets? Or where he could place vending machines for bottled water? None of the above. He was just sitting behind the wheel watching streaming rain, and begging a shrink on the radio to tell him how to motivate himself.

Planning and preparation make money for you. They fuel your confident, positive attitude, and without them, your career will run imperceptibly slower until it crawls into a lay-by.

CALL OBJECTIVES – PRIMARY AND SECONDARY

'Hello, Tony' says the voice on the line 'this is just a courtesy call…'

Wow! Am I agog? Am I on the edge of my seat? Would you be? Do you think I've ever put down the phone and thought 'Well, bless my paws and whiskers! That person was so courteous! We need more courtesy. I think I'll order some'?

If a person has time to make calls like this, there is something fundamentally flabby in their business.

Your job is to make people want what you've got. Those same people are busy. You've got to have an attractive offer or they can't justify making time for you. They didn't walk into their office this morning thinking 'Hey, I wonder what the weather's like in Bexhill-on-Sea? Maybe today I'll get a courtesy call to tell me…'

Don't confuse checking on an order with a courtesy call. If you ring up to confirm that everything on an invoice was delivered safely, that has a purpose, but otherwise what do callers really expect to gain from courtesy calls? I think they're using hope as a strategy.

"I'll call now, at exactly five to ten on Monday morning, because somebody might have mentioned our products only minutes ago, and they might be just thinking right now of placing a big order, and you never know, so…"

Maybe they think that they are keeping themselves at the forefront of the client's mind. Well, they're certainly right there, but if their contact has just twenty-five minutes in which to complete a report for the CEO, and she gets a courtesy call, the forefront of her mind is not bathed in the sweetness and light that they may think.

Every call, either on the 'phone or in person, should have a primary purpose and a secondary purpose. Some of the most successful sales-people I know will often have a tertiary purpose and, let's face it, it's better to have more objectives for a sales call than not enough!

In today's tough climate there will always be a myriad of objectives you should be striving to achieve from any sales call.

Follow my 'Quids In' Formula:

> **Q** – qualify a lead
>
> **U** – unfold a new business opportunity
>
> **I** – identify more people in the DMU
>
> **D** – determine the customer's real needs by the use of 'Conversational Questioning'
>
> **S** – shape your proposition to fit the client and create DESIRE!
>
> **I** – investigate the progress of their implementation of your product/service
>
> **N** – never think your call is simply a courtesy call!

How will you improve your call preparation?

Try this. The North American Indians had an expression which boils down to:

"Before you can truly understand another person you should walk a mile in their moccasins."

So before you make the call take five minutes to build an understanding of what it's like to be the other person. Draw a picture of the kind of shoes they are wearing. (It doesn't matter what your drawing is like. We aren't looking for Da Vinci or Banksy here – you are just creating an image that works for you.) Then around the outside of this image write down as many things as you can that describe what is going on in their world. What are their priorities right now, how are they feeling, what do they see and hear in the seconds before your call arrives? Now focus on the purpose of your call and overlay your purpose into their world. Hear how the conversation goes from their perspective and adjust your approach accordingly.

CHAPTER THREE

GETTING THE INITIAL APPOINTMENT

MAY I, OR MAY I NOT, SPEAK TO THE GREAT KING?

Whether you operate in a field sales role or a telesales role, successful cold calling is all about background, attitude and curiosity. Two people need to welcome you in: first a gatekeeper, next your potential client. The only way you have a hope of engaging their interest is by being confident, knowing a little about them in advance and asking questions that will engage their interest.

But you're not even behind the portcullis of the castle yet. Most of the good questions come later. First you've got to overcome some looming obstacles.

COLD CALLING: SELF-DISCIPLINE

Successful cold calling is not about positive thinking, and I'll tell you why.

Let's say an inexperienced sales-person starts work. This person has a list of numbers, a phone and an aim in mind. Extras like a chair, a prompt sheet, a headset, or workstations occupied by other people are all optional. This person has read a book about positive thinking and has convinced herself that her calls will be politely welcomed and that respondents will be interested in what she has to say. If they're not, they will be won over by her natural talent to persuade.

The outcome? You know the outcome. After fifteen minutes she's introducing herself as though she'd lost the will to live.

'HelloI'mcallingfromAcmeActioninAccringtoncanIspea ktothemanagingdirectorplease.'

After twenty-five minutes she has been urgently interrupted. Somebody's asked her for something or she's hanging out of the bathroom window puffing Bensons into a cold wind or she's waiting for the kettle to boil. Do you think any kind of displacement activity is welcome at this point? Too right. She'd rather clean the toilets (if she could get commission) than go back to that phone.

The biggest single factor making sales-people fail is that they don't discipline themselves to achieve their target number of cold calls. It is hard, but it is the only thing that gets you success. It is the sales-person's equivalent of getting up at five in the morning for a ten-mile run in driving sleet. Ninety percent of the people you call will reject you. The successful sales-people are the ones who seize the ten percent and fill their sales pipelines. Even if they have a terrible day, and by pure bad luck get rejected by everyone they speak to, they'll at least get a feeling of achievement from having done what they had to do.

Persistence makes progress – even if it doesn't feel like it at the time.

Sales-people must shrug off the emotional burden of rejection. It happens. It's part of the job. Pain doesn't make high achievers falter or stop if they're in the *Zenith Zone*. How many parts did Tom Cruise get turned down for before he got his big break? How many books did Michael Crichton write before he produced a bestseller? In any profession that requires persistence the entry qualification is learning not to be dismayed by lack of interest, but to focus on the joy of getting a small step closer to the goal by learning the part, writing the rejected book, making the cold call. Even if it got you nowhere this time, you usually learn something by just doing it. And a good sales-person will maintain focus on the joy of the ten percent (or exceptionally, thirty percent or more) of cold calls who turn into prospects.

Put a sign up: I will not move from this desk until I have made twenty sales calls.

SALES CALLS - MAINTAINING CONTROL

Have you heard "selling is a numbers game"? What do you think people mean by it? I believe they mean the ratio of orders successfully obtained to pitches made. But a one in ten ratio can always be improved. How can you raise it to three, or even four in ten?

You can raise it by taking and keeping control. If you are in control of the sales conversation, your ratio of orders to calls will be higher.

I'll give you an example of control so you know what it feels like. You're going to play a game with another person: the 'one to twenty' game. One of you picks a number to start the game: either one or two. After that all you have to do is take turns in counting upwards in increments of one or two. (So if I began with two, you could say three or four.) The person who gets to twenty first is the winner.

Challenge somebody to play best of three with you. For instance – Tony: two. Jane: three. Tony: five. Jane: seven. Tony: eight. Jane: ten: Tony: eleven. Jane: thirteen. Tony: fifteen. Jane: sixteen. Tony: seventeen. Jane: eighteen: Tony: twenty …

I can win this game every time simply by identifying the controlling numbers, which are: two, five, eight, eleven, fourteen, seventeen. It doesn't matter what my opponent selects as long as I can gain control at some point.

You see? A numbers game; and I'm in control of the outcome. Maintain this control with sales calls, and you're half-way there. I do not for one moment suggest the sales process is as simple as this game but I am suggesting that if you identify and complete everything you need to do at every phase of your sales process you *will* be more in control of the sale and more importantly the outcome!

TWO SIMPLE GOALS FOR COLD CALLING SUCCESS

GOAL 1 - INFORMATION

The biggest thing you want to gain from cold calling is information. Learn who the decision makers are, find out the best time to reach them, get direct dial phone numbers, cell phones, and email addresses. Uncover whether they are using other products, services, or vendors that relate to what you are offering. If they are using a similar product or service, dig to find out if there are current frustrations or areas of opportunity for improvement. I always like to ask something like:

"What things would open the door to have you consider another provider?"

Your primary goal is to get as many details as possible to help qualify the prospect as a viable lead in your database.

GOAL 2 - FOLLOW UP OPPORTUNITIES

Cold calling will almost never get you the deal on the first call. Change your expectation to that of creating follow-up opportunities. This is where you begin to lay the foundation and build a pipeline that will return big time results in the future!

If a prospect is unwilling or unable to talk now, find out a best time to call them back, or try to schedule an appointment to meet at a time when they are expecting you.

Now you have an opportunity to show that you can live up to expectations by making sure that you call back on the day that you promised. The 'cold' part is over. Be dependable and professionally persistent.

When you look back at the end of the day, you might have made twenty, thirty, even forty cold calls and you don't feel like you got anything out of it - mainly because you didn't schedule that many appointments. Maybe you've had a tough couple of days and haven't scheduled any appointments at all.

I suggest looking at it from a completely different perspective. The result of your cold calling effort should be in figuring out how much information you gathered and how many follow-up opportunities you created. Achieving these two goals every day will set you up for the greatest success!

IDENTIFYING THE REAL ENEMY

If you ask sales-people who have to make calls at the start of the sales process, a large number of them will tell you they think the gatekeeper is the enemy. Why? Well getting past gatekeepers is the first big challenge. They have been told not to put unsolicited calls through to the person you are trying to contact, and they won't! It's their job to keep the gate slammed shut. They get paid for it. The larger the organisation the more difficult it is to contact people. Most of them operate a no name policy (which is strange when you consider the gatekeeper always gives theirs!)

Often you are told that the relevant personnel are constantly out, in a meeting, on holiday (back a week on Tuesday but you can leave a message on the voicemail). You can even be told that they would not be interested in your proposition even before you have divulged what your proposition is!

"How can this be?" I hear you ask.

It can be because there are a lot of dire sales-people who offer no differentiation whatsoever and even more alarmingly have no charisma about their call technique. If your product or service has no differentiation in the eyes of any potential buyer it is a commodity product, and unless your price is the lowest you will have little or no chance of winning the business. Gatekeepers play a more important role in today's business environment in protecting the valuable time of decision makers. So the days of making small talk with the person who answers the phone in an attempt to get put through to the relevant procurement manager have long gone.

You need to offer a potential benefit and you must sound professional when you initially speak to the guardian of the decision makers.

Gatekeepers have come in for a lot of bad press from sales-people; they have been called some terrible names. The primary reason is that poor sales-people actually believe that a good gatekeeper is someone who helps them get through to the person they ask for. Well, guess what? They are wrong!

Gatekeepers are doing their job and until we realise this and change our paradigms there is only one enemy: *ourselves*!

This is a key moment in time. We need to be in Peak State and think about what we are going to say to these people. We have to make sure we can be creative because creative sales-people will get the gatekeeper on their side and identify them as an ally.

What will creative sales-people do?

"I've been asked to send some information to your sales director. Could I ask you what's the best way I can do that?"

A percentage of gatekeepers will (if they trust you are telling the truth) give the correct name and address. (The really cunning sales-person never forgets to ask for the postcode and any other details your CRM system requires.)

They'll ring before eight in the morning. This is the time when the decision-maker, having come in early to get some work done uninterrupted, might pick up the phone.

"Would you put me through to the person who's got ultimate responsibility for the sales team?"

"That's me."

They ring late, after normal working hours, and push one or two digits past the main reception number (2002 instead of 2000). They find themselves connected to a decision maker's voicemail.

The next morning they dial the same number!

They also call and say:

"Good morning. I'd like to place an order please."

Guess what – they get put through to the order department.

"Good morning. I'd like to speak to the person responsible for sales training"

"You're in the wrong department."

"Oh I'm sorry. Could you put me through to the right person, or give me the name of the person I need to speak to?"

They are not trained to in the same way as the gatekeeper is, and may well connect you or give you the name you are after!

Very clever but remember this doesn't work every time. You can get re-routed to the gatekeeper!

CHUTZPAH
(DEFINED IN MY DICTIONARY AS 'GUTSY AUDACITY')

Use my ABCD brand of charm...

"Do you mind if I ask you a question?"

"Go right ahead."

"Are you the person responsible for preventing people like me getting through to decision makers?"

"I'm the receptionist."

"I would love the opportunity to demonstrate to you that I am different from the rest."

"How are you going to do that?"

"Well to start with I will be totally honest with you and fully respect your position in the organisation"

"OK, Go On"

"I am not trying to sell you anything, because at this stage I don't know if I have anything you want. All I am trying to do is ascertain whether or not we have a service that would be of value to your company, so could you direct me to the person who is best qualified to make that decision?"

Some will get snappy when you act smart, but some won't. The ones who do – well, you won't try it with them again. And what good cold callers have is a kind of resilience that tells them 'on average, you've got to speak to twenty miserable sods before you find one receptive person.' If a gatekeeper's being awkward, make it obvious you don't take them seriously. When they ask what you've got to be so cheerful about, tell them theirs is another 'No' out of the way – another way to get through the day faster.

We all know how body language is a visual revelation of your attitude. Your voice is even more of a giveaway. Be assertive, but not arrogant! The balance between assertiveness and humbleness is very powerful in the world of sales.

Don't let your voice rise; don't be hesitant. Assert yourself.

"Hello. May I speak to Paul? – It's Tony."

(Oh, first name terms! Better put him through.) Or

"May I speak to the Managing Director?"

"Oh may I ask what it's about?"

"Yes, it's about the ongoing developing people like you."

In my case, that's true, and it usually silences them.

I often get asked when I make a request to speak to a Sales Director:

"Will he know what it's concerning?"

I always reply:

"Yes he will." What I don't say aloud of course is, "After we have spoken!"

After all she did ask will he know not does he know, and I always like to demonstrate my superior listening skills!

Gate keeping can be a licence to bully, and some of them enjoy trying to belittle anyone who's got to ask them for something. Rise above it. Make them feel uncomfortable. Bullies always cave in fast if you refuse to be bullied, and you can only do that if you have the right attitude.

Tactics like this will only work some of the time but, if they facilitate contact with a decision maker in one of the Top 500 companies, they could mean that your company grows tenfold. It really is true that one call, well followed up, can grow a £2m turnover to £20m. The sales-person who made that call will be on such a high that they repeat the success again and again and then try something else. Because now they have proof: nobody is out of the office all the time.

And it is the sales-person's job to get to them.

If we are to succeed we must be different. Because we cannot give up. For us, the rewards are worth all of it.

You have to develop a mentality that aligns your expectations with reality. A good way to do this is to remember the SW SW SW WN mantra – Some Will, Some Won't, So What, Who's Next!

INTERRUPTING FOR A LIVING

"May I ask what it's concerning?"

You resist the impulse to tell this gatekeeper to mind their own damn business, and politely explain what your company, Profitsup & Costsdown, would like to speak to their manager about.

"Oh we're not interested in keeping costs down," they might say.

Pause; sharp intake of breath. You don't believe you are hearing right.

"Would you mind if I obtained some verification from your MD that you are not looking to keep costs down at present?"

You may gently wonder aloud about all sorts of things – like whether she's sure she's qualified to judge what the company's interested in; or whether she's ever made that judgement before, and whether the Managing Director knows.

Gatekeepers are not paid to find out about you and what you can do for the company. They are gatekeepers because they are susceptible to the weight of a heavy boot from above. This susceptibility can work against them if it's suggested subtly and sweetly.

So be ready for your amazement and wonder to take effect. You may get put through to the MD's Personal Assistant, in which case you are interrupting his or her work; or with luck, you will be transferred to the boss and you are doing exactly the same.

Either way your attitude at this stage must be confident. I once read that cold-callers lose more than thirty percent of potential sales once the decision-maker gets on the phone. The figure is probably plucked out of the air but it makes sense, doesn't it? You might think they dry up because they're so astonished at getting through at all. In fact it's because they didn't actually think they would be connected and their preparation is inadequate therefore they don't sound credible or they ask all the wrong questions.

Another illustration of how sales-people have to be in a positive frame of mind at all times.

GETTING THEIR ATTENTION

When you do get through, you have a few precious minutes in which to create demand and reassure your potential customer that you could do business together.

Remember that this first contact may well be inconvenient: you're interrupting for a living.

What have you got to get from them?

Not what you think.

Their attention. Selling is a process you can chunk down, like any other. And the first chunk is: engaging their interest before you start. If you don't, you won't be able to have a two-way conversation, and without that, they won't buy anything!

Think of the many ways you can gain their attention, for example you may ask a killer question,

"Do you mind if I ask what is the biggest challenge representing your procurement department currently?"

You might demonstrate how much research you have conducted on them,

"I understand that you have recently acquired Fleceham and Scarper and are now the leading supplier in the European market."

The key here is to remember that now is not the time to start selling; now is the time to create the right initial impression! So many sales-people start selling too soon, killing any chance of gaining a sale at some point in the future. Initially you need to find out what is going on in your customer's world and establish any areas where there is potential for you to work together.

Focus on them and not *you* and you will have a much better chance of getting their attention.

CHAPTER FOUR

MEETING THE CUSTOMER

CLOSE ENCOUNTERS OF THE SALES KIND.

GET THEIR ATTENTION (IF YOU DON'T YOU ARE NOTHING BUT AN INTERRUPTION!)

One guy used to ring me at the end of every month.

"Hello Mr Dim ... Dim ... Dimidge. How's it going in recruitment?"

I always replied, "I wouldn't know I am not in recruitment."

He would laugh and say, "Have you any vacancies I can help you with?"

He always got my name wrong, and he always persisted in asking me a question that irritated me. What use was that? Call me old-fashioned, but if I'm selling ice, I reckon it helps to know whether or not my prospect is in the fridge business. Not only had he done no research, but he never listened; he had a false laugh. In short, he was not my favourite interruption and, just once, he caught me out of my *Zenith Zone*.

"Do you think," I snarled "that if I'd needed a sales-person I'd have said Ooh, let's wait twenty days until Robert calls me again and asks how things are in recruitment?"

There was a deadly silence...

"Or do you think I would have called the person I wanted to assist me with the search pro-actively?"

If someone has been making fifty calls a day for three months they are inevitably in parrot mode. Sometimes people believe that selling is only a numbers game. As long as they hammer it, it will work, but this is not the case. Selling is also a thinking game, a strategic process, many telesales operatives working at this intensity miss a lot of opportunities, because they have not been given the appropriate training and coaching.

Robert annoyed me because he always said the same things and never listened to my response. If you kick off with a useless remark, you'll get a useless response!

Ever gone out to buy clothes in a shopping centre? You walk into any shop and hear:

"Can I help you?"

"No thanks. I am just looking!" (Except in Brighton where everyone says "Just browsing.")

They walk off.

Ten seconds later you leave the shop.

It can be even more amazing!

You walk into the shop, looking at the shirts or whatever, then the inevitable happens.

"Can I help you?"

"No thanks. I am just looking!"

They walk off.

Yet before they take six steps from you, you call out,

"Excuse me, do you have this in blue?"

So we did want help, they could have helped us, yet we still said "No!"

Why?

Why do you think we react like that?

I believe it is our automatic response to a poor question. It's back to the complacency again. No thought went into the question; it is what they say to everyone that enters the shop. Is that how we engage with people and begin to create rapport?

Throughout the five minutes you've got in which to present your proposition, you need to understand what you are doing because it will give you more control. How many people in sales do that? Very few.

With business to business, it's hard to find out what the stupid question is. You may get a clue from your response rates but certainly wouldn't recommend opening with this question:

"Hello Tony. How are you?"

A cold caller said exactly this to me earlier today. The call was not just from someone I'd never heard of. It was from someone I'd never heard of calling long-distance from Detroit to sign me up for a business charge-card.

"How are you?" Talk about meaningless pleasantries; but of course I'm all heart. Not everyone is.

Far better to say: "Hello Tony (Jane/Aloysius/Sir Humphrey). We haven't spoken before, so thanks for taking my call."

If something in their intonation – or even Happy Birthday being roared in the background – tells you their attention is elsewhere, don't ask: "Are you busy?" because the answer is "Yes."

Just say you hope this is a convenient time. If it isn't, then don't ever say:

"I appreciate that, but this will only take two minutes."

To do so shows disrespect for the person on the other end of the phone. It creates no demand from them, except a resolution never to take a call from you again.

If they are busy, then apologise for interrupting and say:

"I think what I've got to say would be of interest – can I call you later today or tomorrow?" because research has shown that if you give people two choices, they are more likely to take one of them.

If, when you explain that what you have to say would be of interest, they say: "Oh? What is it?" then reply with, "I wouldn't want to go into any detail now you have told me that you're busy."

If they insist: "No, now will be fine," you have taken control; they are doing the asking now.

"Are you sure? How long have I got?" They'll give you five minutes. But earn and respect that five minutes.

Your task now is to build interest. You must therefore turn their attention to something they know well, which relates directly to them and their company; and you must also sound businesslike, as though you have an aim in view rather than a time-wasting chat.

"The purpose of my call is to find out what is currently your biggest business challenge. And how successful you are in overcoming that challenge. Depending on your answer we can discuss whether we can help you."

What we are doing here is creating *focus*. Focus on their issues, focus on the possibility that you have a solution, focus on hearing more, *not* how fast they can kill the call.

Why is focus important? Focus is important for 2 reasons:

1) Because you get what you focus on, and
2) Because focus creates curiosity ...

"What would it mean to you if we could solve that problem for you?"

"What would it mean to your company? ...Your department? ...You?"

Think about the last time you considered changing your car. You had a particular make and maybe even a model in mind. Do you remember that suddenly there were a lot of them around?

There weren't really more of them around; it's simply that you are now focussed on that make and model and then you got curious: who had the sports alloys, what were the interior options, which colours looked the best...

And it's the same when we talk to customers. So, think carefully about what you want your customer to focus on: killing the call as fast as possible or focussing on what value you might be able to add and to help them get curious about that.

At this stage your background research and the questions you are asking about this company are beginning to form some sort of picture of their issues. If your aim is to go and meet them, you may not at this early stage be able to recognise the features, advantages and benefits of your product or service which will be of particular interest to them, so it's better not to tell them much; what is an advantage or benefit to one won't be to another, and it is important to recognise this. They are doing the talking at this stage, and you're saving many of the questions until later.

In my first year of cold calling, I learned to listen carefully to the implications behind responses, scribble notes and seize opportunities. If, like me, you're offering a service that will increase profits, you may hear:

"What would it mean to me?"

Well, it would be great for me personally, because my boss is leaving in six months and it would put me in line for his job.

Here is your opportunity to attach yourself to this person's situation and demonstrate your desire to be part of the solution.

"Then we should meet and talk, because I would be delighted to invest some time to explore how my proposition could help you to achieve your goal..."

Bang! You have created some initial demand. Another thing you can do is make a big bold claim. I once met a man with a fantastic business card: his company and his name were on it, and a photograph of himself laughing. He told me that people often ask why he's laughing on the picture, and he asks them back:

"What do you think you're going to be doing when I tell you what I can do for your business?" He said it gets their attention. You'll notice how it also gives him control of the situation.

What works for one person won't for another. It's our job to find things that put us in control – that work at least ten percent of the time for us – and a well-rehearsed plan for what we say when they do. In my first year, I would often start speaking quickly and cheerfully:

"Hi – before you say a single word this is a sales call. If you want to put the phone down feel free to do so now."

"Why would I want to do that?"

"I dunno but the last four people have."

"Oh. Tell me more…"

Bang! Got some initial interest thanks to differentiation and positivity.

Put the fun back into what you do.

BEGIN WITH THE END IN MIND

You've battled your way past the gatekeeper and now you've got five minutes of the decision-maker's time. Does it feel as if you're on the verge of reaching your goal? Don't kid yourself. You've just slain a few dragons. The ultimate goal is way off, and here's a big test. You'll sail through it, though, if you've prepared yourself.

Do you know exactly why you are calling?

Do you want to send them sales literature? Do you want to make an appointment to go and see them? Do you want to find out what they want and send them a quote there and then?

Begin:

"The purpose of my call is …"

Let's say it's

"… to introduce our services and see if your company has a need for any of them,"

"What are you selling?"

"I'm not selling anything until I've established that you need something."

"That's refreshing... Can you give me a clue?"

"According to my research you've got a sales team of 150 people."

"Yes."

"Can you tell me if you've ever invested in any training?"

"Yes."

"That's the sort of business I'm with. I'd like to find out what sort of training you've invested in, how well your current suppliers are doing, and what could be done better."

You are being open, honest and *different*! People often respond:

"OK. Make an appointment to come along and see me."

If your aim is to make an appointment, don't be drawn into a description of your services over the telephone.

"All I'm trying to do is make an appointment,"

"What's it about?"

"Sales training,"

"Sounds good, tell me more."

The foolish sales-person thinks Saint Lucy has smiled. And then it all pours out. Big mistake!

Telling isn't selling. Telling is just telling. Your objective at this stage is not to inform, but to get attention and interest. If you tell them everything, they will let you bang on for five minutes and then tell you they are not interested. They can put the phone down and you've lost them for good. Buyers read books about handling people like us.

You are not the only loser in this situation. They'll have wasted five minutes of their time listening, which they could have spent in identifying what they really need.

Don't be drawn. Begin with the end in mind, and keep it in mind at all times.

KEEPING YOUR GUARD UP

*A*ttitude, *B*ackground, and *C*uriosity will get you into a situation where you can create *D*emand – but only if you're prepared to use your defences at every turn. You will be challenged, even at this early stage in your relationship with the potential buyer, by objections. So you need to be prepared for them, otherwise you won't get your sale.

The first thing you need to create is an automatic response to a negative reaction.

If you are armed with a polite and interested response to a negative answer, you have the chance to progress the call despite the initial negative reaction. If you are not, and they're unenthusiastic, you will either give up, or feel deflated and start wittering - um, actually, basically: or you'll be all bravado and start telling them "You should" which turns them off.

My response to a negative is a calm:

"You must have a very good reason for saying that: do you mind if I ask what it is?"

For other businesses it might be:

"You must have a very good reason for/not wanting to see the samples/not wanting to consider this until next spring (or whatever)."

You are still building the relationship while praising their judgement, and at worst you're seizing the opportunity to do some market research.

I DON'T KNOW

If you master the art of conversational questioning you will almost certainly be told by some people "I don't know." There are many reasons why people will say this: maybe they don't know, maybe they don't want to tell you, maybe they are not 100% sure of the answer.

There is a great phrase you can use in situations like this, which is:

"If you did know what would you guess?"

You are probably thinking at this point, "Mmmm, I don't like that, it doesn't make sense," but please believe me … IT WORKS!

I have tried it more times than I can remember and nine times out of ten I get an answer. I urge you to be open minded about this and try it out with friends and family: you will be amazed at the results.

TACTICAL WITHDRAWAL

It used to be said that, on average, buyers say "no" six times before they say "yes"; and, on average, most sales-people give up after the third "no".

So what are the "no's" that really mean "no" to most of us? How can we bow out gracefully if we have to, and turn them into a "yes" at a later date?

The first is some variant of:

"No thanks. We're perfectly satisfied with our current supplier."

In the first year after starting my company, I spoke to a really nice local man who had been in business for twenty years, and from the day he'd opened up he'd used a local training organisation. I told him I wasn't surprised that he'd stuck with them because they've got an excellent record. He said:

"That's not good news for you."

"What d'you mean?" I said. "It's great news for me to know there are loyal people out there, because everyone says loyalty doesn't exist anymore. What kind of car do you drive?"

"A seven series BMW."

"What d'you keep in the boot?"

"A spare tyre."

"Why do you carry that?"

"Because it's a legal requirement – I've never used it though."

"That doesn't matter," I said. "Let us be your spare tyre. Just get our systems talking to each other. Put my name on your database and, if ever your supplier can't help, you've got a spare tyre. We're not going to ring you every week but you've a contingency plan. Just let me have your card and details, and we'll get an account set up." It was a huge success. He's never spent a penny with us, but he's told many other people how great we are and they've come to us. He speaks highly of us in many places. So the stock response for a tactical withdrawal from that situation is:

"You may not need us now, but one day, when your regular supplier can't help, you will." Every so often you call the person, just to maintain contact, and sure enough, the day usually comes when they've got an emergency.

Do you respond positively or negatively to a challenge? That's what it comes down to. Rise to it.

A second objection that floors a lot of sales-people is:

"Sorry, we're really not interested."

So often I hear:

"Well if somebody's not interested there's not a lot you can do, is there?" And the sales-people who say this are talking about their major revenue stream, so they really need to beef up their responses. If you've drawn on all your reserves of charm, wit and nerve to get past the gatekeeper and get into a major organisation, why give up now? If you are nineteen years old, it's two in the morning and you're clubbing, and the person you've got your eye on seems too cool to talk to you, do you give up trying and spend the rest of the night propping up a wall? Of course you don't. First establish the basics about the company. If you have researched the background well enough to know that they have preferred supplied lists or an in-house service, you can get that out of the way first by explaining that you know, but you may still be able to offer them something.

Are they genuinely 'not interested' for technical reasons (they don't use BT-subscribed phone lines, for instance), staff reasons or some other perfectly sensible excuse? If so, you can mentally review why that wasn't apparent from your initial research, and then make a dignified retreat.

Otherwise – if there is no apparent impediment to your glorious union – let them know you understand they're not interested. Then, try a different strategy to create a spark of interest.

First you gain agreement to ask more questions:

"Do you mind if I ask you a question?"

"No."

"What would somebody like me have to do to gain your initial interest?"

Ask something like this because, if they have stated that they've no interest, there is no point in continuing the call or calling again unless you can find out what you need to do in order to generate some interest.

You could even try… "You must have a very good reason for saying that. Do you mind if I ask what that is?"

"We're just not interested."

"Do you mind if I ask which one are you not interested in? Is it the broadband service, or the whole telephone package?"

"Umm – I don't know."

"Well if you did know, what would you guess?"

"Umm – the phones."

"Oh I see. So you could be interested in a new broadband supplier?"

"I'm not sure."

"Would you mind putting me through to someone who does?"

I have to say that a person who doesn't have a confident, assertive attitude shouldn't be let loose to sell. Customers identify the sales-person as the company he works for and the brand. Not only that, but the annoyance and time wasting potential of bad sales calls can't be underestimated. If switchboard operators spend most of their day fielding the verbal equivalent of junk mail, how popular are the most frequent junk callers? What are they doing for their company's reputation? Cold calling is a great sales tool – in the right hands.

The third excuse for a 'no' is:

"We don't need (a new phone supplier/business chargecards/500 reams of laser paper)."

Again, you need to find out what exactly they mean by this. If they don't use printers, 'phones or money' there may be an excuse, but otherwise there isn't. What they mean is:

"We don't want to talk to you because we are getting on fine and have other things to think about."

This is a perfectly fair position. It's up to you to develop their curiosity to a point where they start thinking that their 'phones/printers/financial arrangements' may require attention after all. You return to:

"You must have a very good reason for saying that. Do you mind if I ask what it is?"

And:

"I'm surprised you said that since you told me that speed/cost/efficient tracking was really important..."

And so on until they are identifying for themselves the pluses and minuses of their current position, recognising that there may be someone out there who could give them a better deal, and they're talking to that person.

If they appear to have an identifiable need for your product but still don't want to engage with you, switch modes and get personal.

"Listen, I'm outside my comfort zone in saying this – do you mind if I ask you – is it me? Is it something I've said that's made you feel uncomfortable about using our product?"

People are human.

"No!" they'll cry, "It's not you!" and they'll go on to tell you the truth: the one thing that was bothering them all along.

The only insurmountable objection is when there is a genuine drawback.

Their current supplier is the decision maker's brother in law, for instance. This is a definite No-No, so you will have to leave the field – but not without leaving a calling card. So let them know that you empathise and fully understand the situation, and then suggest you make an agreement that, if anything changes, they'll contact you. (Remember my 'Spare Tyre'? 'The last thing I want to do is keep contacting you every month. If you are happy for me to do so, I'll just get in touch every 6 months.' (you never know, the divorce rate being what it is… No, don't say that!)

If the genuine drawback is, "I have to get [widgets] down to a specific unit price." don't ring off; this may not be as final it seems.

Question why. Probe and identify their priorities. Establish the 'Dominant Buying Motive'. There might be a chance you can change the product specification and give them what they want nearer to their price. Theirs is an objection all right, but one that is often easy to handle positively.

Never give up.

The combination of tenacity, questioning, listening and capturing is very powerful. Get customers to think hypothetically about solutions. If a customer told you the most important thing for them is something which nobody in your field yet supplies, and two years later you are the sole supplier (and thanks to your excellent customer relations management system you are able to come back and offer it at almost any price), suddenly you are using their information to make your proposition more powerful. You've got a positive attitude; you've used your background material – the notes you made after your initial contact, and your customer management database; you've used your curiosity; and you have identified the real source of demand.

I think you'll get the gig, don't you?

PITFALLS

You've met the new client. You've done business with them pretty regularly. You think you know about them. But how up-to-date is your understanding? You cannot afford to let your interest lapse. You have to keep up with developments in their business.

Part of the reason sales-people don't always apply themselves is that every day they work alone and don't see a manager. At worst, the only time they have a full and frank exchange of views is when their results are slipping. Two problems can emerge from this isolation. First, they may find it hard to maintain a highly motivated attitude. Second, they get less assiduous about keeping up background research. And unless you can predict what your customers are likely to do next, you won't be ready to expand your service to them as they move forward.

As a sales-person, you'll have to make your calls. But you will also have to keep up-to-date notes. Ever tried to do that a week later? You might as well not bother. Make legible retrievable notes within minutes of the call or the visit. File them in a preparation folder, on a computer or on paper. Scrawl them on a paper napkin if you must, but write them at once and file them properly as soon as you can.

These notes will be invaluable later when you come to write proposals and reports and fill in questionnaires for marketing departments. Weeks after the cold call, when you're on your way to a first visit and can barely remember the original approach you made, you'll be only too glad of those a few sheets of background and the brochure they've sent you.

Often the most outgoing and confident sales-people are the worst organisers. A person who's a natural at schmoozing new clients isn't necessarily smart at maintaining up-to-date background notes. It's not only about slack organisation, either; it's about time-wasting – overdoing the joshing and small talk. Kidding about rival football teams or golf handicaps oils the wheels of acquaintanceship, but keep it to a minimum. These people are not your friends. They are seeing you, and you them, in order to effect transactions which will make you both happy. You're here to spread a little financial sunshine, not to update them on traffic conditions on the M23.

You see how it can all go horribly wrong if you're too complacent? First you create accounts and a full sales pipeline. Then you become an account manager, and get too grand to cold call. You know your clients well enough to take them for granted ... but if the accounts disappear you've nothing left to manage.

It will pay you to sacrifice some selling time to maintaining a background file on every client. If anyone tries to persuade you otherwise, smile politely and shift a little further along the bench.

INSIDE THE CASTLE

You can't relax; you've been invited into the company, and the greatest tests of your skill are yet to come. So don't drop your guard when you get inside the gate.

Firms have become leaner in the last decade. It's not uncommon for the person you've come to see to collect you from Reception. This means you won't get an opportunity to make an entrance with your usual sunny smile and ready handshake. When key personnel first see you, you'll be loitering. Not exactly a high impact situation, but you have to make the best of it.

And don't make the mistake of assuming that 'Sarah,' the person who comes to collect you, is some menial whose views the boss ignores. Assume nothing.

What will you be doing, down there in the foyer? If you are slumped in a chair, picking your nose while puzzling over the Sun crossword, what kind of impact will you have? Better to put your bag on a chair and remain standing, if there is anything at all to study on the walls or out of the window. If not, sit down and briskly scan the material on the coffee table, especially their own material. Don't get too engrossed in the inside pages of the broadsheets or you risk letting all fifty-eight pages of the Daily Telegraph slither to the floor when your host whirls into view.

Then you're in the lift, and having to make conversation. Differentiate yourself by asking about their business, of which you've grasped the broad outlines from preparation. If you're talking to the assistant, don't patronise by assuming that he or she knows nothing.

Get their attention (again).

Your eyes are closed; you are lying on warm sand, in the shade of a palm tree. Waves whisper along the shore. You can hear distant laughter and conversation and the chink of glasses from a beach bar. A gentle breeze sways the branches high above.

HOOT-HOOT-HOOT-HOOT-HOOT-HOOT-HOOT

Aagh! A car alarm.

Back in an English November, we're working. We have an appointment with Jean Smith at 11am. We are in the foyer two minutes early, and what is Jean Smith probably doing? Finishing off a bit of work? Or preparing for her meeting with you? Oh come on – she's forgotten the time. She may even have forgotten you're coming.

You got her attention three weeks ago when you made the appointment. Now you've got to do it again – because when you arrive, you are an interruption.

Do people like being interrupted?

It's shocking, the things careers advisors don't tell you.

"Have you ever thought of a career in Sales? It's a great job: all you have to do is interrupt people!"

European and especially British managers are so busy that even when you have a confirmed appointment and arrive on time they are still busy doing something when you get there. They're thinking I wish I had another ten minutes to finish this off... So we need to make ours a good interruption. After all it's what we do for a living!

Go in with a smile and the kind of positive body language that shows you are in the *Zenith Zone*. And ask good questions - because until you get somebody's attention, you are still an interruption. Good questions are the ones that make them focus on what they really, really want.

THE FIRST MEETING

Your aim, at the first meeting, is to get face to face with a decision-maker; but if this is a big organisation, you may find yourself talking not to the Field Marshal, but to one of the Colonels plucked from the battle lines. Your aim is to get face to face with someone who can make a buying decision. Whether or not they personally can buy what you're selling, your immediate task is to get this first contact on side.

You have fifteen minutes, a carefully thought-out plan of what you need to know, and questions structured so as to give you that information and involve the potential customer, in whatever guise this person appears.

They're just dying to work with you – and then you ask what their buying process is. (Subtext: how are decisions made? Can the person in front of you sign your contract and sanction payment and is that all there is to it? Or are you schmoozing someone who can't take a buying decision even though they want to?)

Now it all comes pouring out. Someone high up the pecking order is a bit of a bully, who has told a second person to get this stuff sorted – and this second person has parked the problem with the person you're talking to.

You come along and lead the person to a correct identification of the problem and a possible solution.

Do you now let him wave you goodbye, rush up to a floor and eagerly describe your possible solution to his immediate superior?

No, you do not. It's like the game of Chinese whispers: the more frequently a message is passed from person to person, the more it gets distorted. Besides, in a hierarchy, too few people are capable of swallowing their pride and accepting a suggestion from a subordinate.

What you will have to do is be there to present the solution in person to the decision-maker at the top.

But you can't just ask nicely for an invitation because you may get turned down. You need to ratchet up demand a little more.

So you might say to your new contact:

"If we could solve this for you, what impact would that have on your business?"

"It would certainly improve our sales/speed of distribution/image with pre-teens."

"What impact would it have on you? Personally?"

"Well, my boss, who is hard to please, would say I've solved the problem. It would be fantastic for me."

And then you could ask:

"What do you think the problems are here?"

"I'll get a proposal from you and I'll take it to my boss and my boss will take it to the Head of Sales/Distribution/Early Learning and she's going to pick holes in it."

This person has been there before. He or she is already feeling uncomfortable at the prospect of a dismissive response.

"Okay," you say, "why don't we devise a solution here?"

You are not going to allow this person to present your proposal. You are not going to let him/her do your job by proxy, because why would you employ a salesperson who is in a subordinate position and dreading failure from the outset?

If anyone is going to be able to sell the proposal, it's you. You have just led your new-found friend to arrive at this conclusion, too. So now you fly to the rescue.

"How would you like it if you got your boss and the Head of Sales/Big Cheese together, and we went through the proposal? But you must tell them you have insisted that I should make the presentation myself, in order to answer any questions they may have."

This is pretty good, because it makes this person seem assertive. In fact the person is gleefully thinking that you're not only going to overcome one of their biggest challenges, but are going to sell it to their superiors and field the flak, if there is any. They'll love you to bits for that.

Leave them alone to be your mouthpiece, and it'll be:

"Hmph," says the head suit, "I'm not sure about that …"

"Oh I know, I did tell them. But they insisted…"

So they'll be working against you.

So where you can, identify the role of the person you're selling to and work out whether there are people higher up in the decision-making chain that you should be talking to. Avoid letting people do your job for you.

Customers shop about. More than ever they have people in and assess competitive proposals. When they say "no" to you, they do so for quite some time. Give them a really compelling proposition at a high enough level, and they'll talk next time even if they don't give you the work on this occasion.

Suggest an agenda!

If you really want to show why you are different think about sending an agenda a few days prior to the meeting. There are a few tricks you can use with agendas that really make the difference.

- Include a purpose in the title.
- Make every agenda item a question (see the next chapter)
- Give each agenda item a time

Here is an example:

Meeting between T.Dimech and P.Wright of Smithsons

Purpose: The purpose of this meeting is to determine …

1. What are the current business challenges? (10 mins)
2. What would fixing these mean to a) you and b) the business? (15 mins)
3. How might we support you in these things? (20 mins)
4. Review and next steps (10 mins)

By adding times, your customer will get a really clear view of how long the meeting will take and what is to be covered giving them a focus and puts you in control of the meeting.

Imagine what this would do for your professionalism and credibility.

BEWARE: Never put 'Any other business' on an agenda. This just gives people an excuse to hijack the meeting and follow their own agenda.

AVOIDING THE SALES-PERSON'S SNAKE: DON'T LET THE BOA BITE YOU!

Normally if you have a well rehearsed questioning strategy you'll speak at a pace that makes people listen and respect what you say. You will monitor your own approach and the points you make will be remembered. Good, attention-getting speakers pace themselves carefully.

However, if you are nervous, it's totally different!

Ever heard a nervous, defensive PR person on the radio?

"Well *obviously* the problem with that approach is that it's *actually* impossible to do, but *obviously* there will be moments when this changes *or whatever* but *basically*, this it isn't within the company's remit."

Basically, Obviously, and Actually are verbal tics like *You Know* and *Or Whatever*, that cover up moments of panic when you are talking too fast and just want to fill up the air with the sound of your own voice because you are trying to disguise your nerves!

Well basically, it's obvious that you're scared out of your wits, actually.

I am not trying to eradicate these words from the English language, but I am urging you to ensure you are not guilty of using them too often in your sales routines!

High, hurried speech sounds nervous, as if the speaker has something to hide. Fast high-pitched delivery combined with verbal tics reveals a defensive mind-state. We instinctively know it represents retreat from opposition. It is the verbal equivalent of taking a step back and putting the hands up submissively. It invites the listener to attack and pursue.

You want to be hustled off the phone or out of their office by irate customers? Raise your voice to a squeak and talk reallyreallyfast and say, obviously, a lot, and see what happens.

CHAPTER FIVE

QUESTIONING SKILLS

THE MOST UNDER-UTILISED SKILL IN THE SALES TOOL BOX: ASK BETTER QUESTIONS

I once went on a course run by Anthony Robbins, the motivational trainer. It was an awesome experience. One thing he said was:

"If you want better sales, learn how to ask better questions."

In fact he went on to say that, if you want to improve any element of your life, learn how to ask better questions.

That changed me. I adopted an interest in a new anorak sport: Asking Questions. I've read more books about questions than I care to admit. I put 'questions' into Google and read what it throws up. I read a book years ago that I believe Harry Enfield read before he created Kevin and Perry. Were you ever Kevin or Perry? I was. My daughter was – until I read a book about questioning skills.

This book suggested it was the parents' fault: there is no such thing as useless children – only useless parents -

and there is no such thing as useless sales-people - just managers who didn't train them adequately.

You need to develop them up or develop them out if they can't do the job.

So instead of asking the parenting equivalent of 'Can I help you?' I had to start asking my children some meaningful questions. At this time my own daughter was Kev'n'Perry, combined.

This is what happens: they come home and the parent says, "Did you have a good day at school?"

Even if they did, would a teenager admit to it? Rubbish question, so they go upstairs.

Two steps up – and another one follows:

"Have you got any homework?"

"Duh. Of course I've got homework I've just been to school." Just let me get to my room and get away from all this. As they get into their room and shut the door a gentle knock precedes the third gem:

"What do you want for tea?"

"Sausages."

"Well I've cooked a nice stew to warm you up."

"Uh! Why ask me what I want for tea when you've already cooked stew?"

Ninety-nine percent of children (in a scientific study conducted in our street) get asked the same three rubbish questions.

I know I did. And as a parent, I asked the same things.

So having read the book I said:

"Hiya!"

And she grunted, and I said:

"Anyone get caught taking drugs in school today?"

"What?"

"You told me somebody had."

Dramatic sigh, eyes rolled to heavens, saintly patience with the poor old fart.

"No, I didn't Dad. I said somebody rolled a joint at half past six outside school and the police drove past and caught them."

Pause. I said:

"Tell me, if you could have put a hash teabag in a teacher's tea today, which teacher would it have been?"

"Dunno."

"Go on," I said, "If you did know, who would you choose?"

"My maths teacher ..." (See it *does* work!)

This idiot had made her stand on a chair. She'd asked a question and he had made her stand on a chair in front of thirty-six children and say:

"One day I will have a desire to learn."

Suddenly we were talking after school and more importantly had learned something. Then I thought: *I wonder if this would work with my wife?*

I used to come home to:

"Have you had a good day? How did it go? Have any orders?"

Same three questions. The cue for me to grunt and fall into a chair, feet up in front of the television. You see how it goes? The minute we get close to somebody we lose the desire to think carefully about what we want to say. Non-communication: how many divorces are caused by that?

We ask the same questions every time we see them!

The problem is whenever we develop a relationship, any relationship, a loving relationship, a parental relationship even a business relationship, the longer we are in it the more complacent we become. The less effort we devote to it.

ICEBERG QUESTIONING

As you are well aware most of the iceberg sits beneath the water line and is not clearly visible. This is the view most sales-people have of their customers because they only ask the obvious questions about their basic needs and requirements: establish the hidden needs and you gain access to a higher level of information than your competitors.

QUESTIONING SKILLS

Telling isn't selling. Telling makes a customer think when will he shut up? Most British salesmen are too anxious to give information that hasn't been asked for.

Should you tell them what you do?

Or should you ask them what they need?

Research on successful selling shows that the questioning or 'consultative' style is the most successful approach to a sale. Just as it's a highly successful approach to teaching. Good salesmen and good teachers have two things in common. One is the ability to engage an audience by asking the right questions.

The other is the ability to impart information while asking a question!

Were you aware that ostriches don't bury their heads in the sand? If not, you've just learned something – and all I did was ask you a question.

You do this automatically on the phone. Let's say your company prints designs onto fabric. Somebody rings up to ask whether you can print two hundred tee-shirts – and you're to supply the tee-shirts. The first thing you do is identify exactly which permutations on the basic tee-shirt they want.

"I'm pretty sure we can supply you. Did you know we stock five different fabrics and men's and women's sizes in thirty colours, five shapes, and three sleeve lengths?"

"Great."

"May I run through the options with you so that we can identify exactly what you need?"

You will find out how many extra-large tee-shirts they want in crimson lycra with long sleeves and, as you do so, you are breaking down the conversation into chunks. You offer a choice of fabric and your client asks you to explain the differences; and so it goes on. You're both engaged, and you're building rapport as your questions bring into focus what it is that the customer really needs.

BEYOND 'OPEN' & 'CLOSED'

Most of you will understand the difference between 'Open' questions and 'Closed' questions. Just in case there is any doubt I recall Rudyard Kipling's opening lines of 'I Keep Six Honest …'

I keep six honest serving-men
(They taught me all I knew);
Their names are What and Why and When
And How and Where and Who.
I send them over land and sea,
I send them east and west;
But after they have worked for me,
I give them all a rest.

I am sure Kipling would have made a great sales-person, not only did he appreciate the importance of open questions; he knew when to shut up!

'Open' questions are a great way to gain information and open people up, 'Closed' questions are answered with one of two possibilities, "*yes*" or "*no*."

Do not make the mistake of classifying closed questions as bad questions; they do have their time and place as we will discover later in this book. However open questions are generally a much better option.

BEYOND 'OPEN' & 'CLOSED': 5 POWERFUL QUESTIONING STRATEGIES

I would like to introduce to you six sub-classifications of open questions, which will help you master the art of asking better questions:

- Reflective Questions
- Hypothetical Questions
- Challenging Questions
- Commitment Building Questions

And the sales-persons best friend …

- Alternative Choice Questions

Let's look at these in more detail.

REFLECTIVE QUESTIONS

Reflective questions are based on the content of previous answers, they are psychologically powerful because they 'reflect' something the other person has said or feels and provides some proof of your empathy and listening skills.

Example: "You mentioned earlier that you wanted to offer tee shirts in ten colours, how important is that to you?"

HYPOTHETICAL QUESTIONS

Hypothetical questions create an image of the future, used correctly they position you in that picture.

Example: "If you were to go ahead with this project where do you see it having the biggest impact?"

CHALLENGING QUESTIONS

Some customers can exaggerate; we have to be very careful how we respond to this, so by simply repeating the key word we can challenge them in a non confrontational manner, and often enable them to realise their exaggeration without feeling silly.

Example: "I dealt with your company once before, but they never invoiced me correctly."

"*Never?*"

"Well, there were a number of errors …"

COMMITMENT BUILDING QUESTIONS

You may want to ask a question to encourage the customer to increase their level of commitment.

Example: "Would you like us to incorporate your company's livery into the software, if you were to proceed?"

If you get a 'yes' to this you know there is some commitment and it is worthwhile investing some more time.

ALTERNATIVE CHOICE QUESTIONS

If this technique is mastered you get more people accepting one of the choices you offer them. Example: "Would you like delivery before Christmas or after Christmas?"

It doesn't matter which one they choose - you have the business.

Restaurants have learnt that if you ask a closed question, like "Would you like some water?" there is a fifty percent chance of a 'no'! However if you ask "Would you like still or sparkling?" many more people choose one. In fact in some cases they end up selling *both*.

You see the power of this sort of questioning strategy? Will you start to incorporate it into your sales routine tomorrow or next week?

CONVERSATIONAL QUESTIONING

Having this ammunition in the guise of questioning power is great, but there is a potential danger, turning your meeting into an interrogation!

I have seen many sales-people tell me they are going to focus on their questioning skills at the next meeting and wonder on the way out why they failed to achieve their call objectives. In most cases the reason is the same one - they turned the meeting into an interrogation.

You need to focus on creating an atmosphere where the other person is relaxed and comfortable; if you do this and ask the right questions they will be happy to talk about their world and the challenges they face. If you just ask an endless stream of questions, however well constructed they are, you will not get the same result.

Try to aim to get the other person talking for eighty percent of the time and also try to ensure that in your twenty percent of the conversation you spend eighty percent asking questions.

Now get your mind focus back to your work environment and think of some questions in each category that would help you progress a sale:

1) Reflective Questions
2) Hypothetical Questions
3) Challenging Questions
4) Commitment Building Questions
5) Alternative Choice Questions

CHAPTER SIX

CREATING DESIRE

GIVE THEM WHAT THEY WANT WHAT THEY REALLY, REALLY WANT

 I want to start this chapter by asking you to think about desire. Think what desire in business is. More importantly think of what you need to do as a salesperson in order to create desire for your proposition.

- What is your definition of DESIRE?
- What do you need to do in order to create desire?

We've all done it; gone shopping with nothing but an ill-defined idea (usually for something domestic and expensive that we don't often buy, like a new kitchen floor). Yet we've come home having bought the perfect solution that was right within our budget. And most of the time, our attention was drawn to this item by the kind of effective selling that focussed our own ideas on what we really wanted and created demand for it. How important would this be in selling the house for us? How important was a lifetime guarantee? How important was the disruption of having the floor laid? These are some of the things the sales-person, or the sales literature, asked us to evaluate and, as we did, we talked about the size of the kitchen and frequency of olive oil spillage, and gained confidence that she was getting a complete picture of the situation and could be trusted to direct us, out of her greater knowledge of what was on offer, towards the ideal solution.

How many people in business really know what they want to buy? Very few. Buying decisions here are made like any other. Good sales-people help the buyer to define exactly what their priorities are (creating demand) and give them confidence that they are getting the best advice and making the correct decision (reassurance). You use your proposition to help buyers realise 'This is what is right for my business.' They haven't been sold to; they've been helped. They're happy, the way anyone is who's made a wise purchase.

As the sales process proceeds, your customers may be surprised by the degree of understanding you've gained about the way they work. Above all they must feel they can trust their own judgement about buying from you.

I once found this out just in time.

I was driving up the motorway; it was about three years ago, and I had to go up north for an early morning meeting. We'd presented our proposal in competition with five other training companies, and we'd been told we were in the final two. I can listen to music on the motorway or I can think; so I thought.

I asked myself if this potential client would ask me to drive for two hours to say "Thanks but no thanks," or "Thanks, we'll hire you."

No, he wouldn't. Therefore there must be a hidden agenda. Maybe he'd thought of a question he hadn't asked before – like:

"What if we train our sales force and they're all brilliant, and then they leave to work for the competition?" I've had to answer that one often enough. What if he doesn't train them, and they stay?

Or he might want to reduce the numbers.

Price was the most likely reason for the meeting.

So I decided to take a risky strategy that would demonstrate our professionalism. Sure enough, he began with the good news: we had the job.

"Great, " I said. "You've made a good decision."

"But what can you do on the price?"

"That's good news too," I said. "I will give you what you really want! So with immediate effect I propose a price increase of 5%."

I could see the muscles in his neck working. I said:

"I know you think I'm taking liberties, but please give me two minutes."

He nodded, teeth clenched.

"You've asked me to quote for a negotiation skills course for seventy of your sales-people, right?"

"Yes."

"A two-day residential course, seven times, with ten people each time, and I am going to stay overnight in the hotel with them. Seven times, we'll have dinner together and I'll see them at breakfast."

"Yes."

"Do you think at least once on these occasions somebody will ask how I got the business?"

"I suppose so."

"How would you prefer me to answer that question? By saying as soon as you asked for a discount I crumbled and gave you one, or would you prefer me to tell them that I had the balls to look you in the face and ask for a five percent increase?"

He was silent for a moment as he thought about my questions then answered:

"You're good, and what's more you are right!"

I kept the order, and I got the increase.

"But," he said, "on one condition, you don't put an increase on it next year."

I thought great! I've got the business next year as well.

It's true that I was in a strong position to start with because I already had the order. But the reason I was able to take this bold position is that I'd presented successfully, but I hadn't at previous meetings had the opportunity to identify what he really, really wanted. Only thinking about it, on the way up in the car, I had.

He didn't really want a price reduction; he really wanted reassurance that he'd chosen somebody who'd do a brilliant job with his sales staff.

To this day, I'm the only sales trainer he uses; I am one of the few suppliers who gets invited to their annual conference. He still tells this story to his members of staff, and admits now that in the cold light of day he would have thought less of me if I'd rolled over.

Put all the time you've got into thinking about what they really, really want. This will minimise objections and enable you to overcome them in a creative, professional manner.

SALESMAN'S POKER

I spoke in depth in the previous chapter about the importance of questions, and in terms of differentiation there are two reasons why:

Your style will differentiate you from your competitors and create more demand.

You can now use the information you gained to create a unique proposition that is shaped around the individual requirements of your customer, creating even more desire!

I have heard many sales-people give away all of the features, advantages and potential benefits in their proposition in one fell swoop, without pausing to gauge the customer's reaction to anything. I think the poker approach is one to bear in mind here. Give a small amount of information (select which element by digesting the information you gained when asking questions) and see how much desire that has created first.

For example: "You mentioned earlier that results are important to you in relation to your SEO page rankings; you will probably be pleased to hear that we charge a flat fee for our service and the remainder is aligned to an agreed results schedule. If we don't deliver you don't pay! Does that sound fair to you?"

Just deliver the proposition in small chunks and monitor the impact each one has on your customer. Don't show all your hand at once and expect them to bite your hand off.

Remember – Telling Isn't Selling!

CHAPTER SEVEN

PRESENTING YOUR PROPOSAL

PRESENTING THE PROPOSAL. WHAT DO PEOPLE BUY?

People buy people! Yes, people. OK, they buy products and services they want, at prices they are happy to pay, from brands they trust but they usually buy them from people.

Many British companies spend hundreds of thousands, even millions, defining their brand in the public mind, and then hand over their baby to some entirely inappropriate sales-person. If you'd sum up your brand as design-led, contemporary and innovative, would you send it out on the road with some guy in a dandruffy suit who licks the stub of his pencil before he fills in the order book? It happens, believe me.

American companies call their sales-people Reps. We should call ourselves the same, to remind us that we represent the brand we're selling.

How many times have you made a decision to buy something, went out to make the purchase and ended up not buying it because you couldn't stand the way you were being sold to, or the person selling to you?

On the other hand, how many times have you bought something because you were influenced by the quality and calibre of the sales-person?

As sales-people we generally respect other sales-people. We are easy to sell to if the person selling to us is doing what we consider to be a "good Job". However, we don't tolerate bad selling: sales-people who overwhelm you with unsolicited information, or who try to close regardless of what we might need, or whose response to objections is dismissive.

A sales presentation is your opportunity to let potential or existing clients know just how professional you are, how much you have established about their need by asking better questions than your competitors, how you have shaped your proposal around their individual needs, and how you have carefully prepared to deliver that proposal to them.

THE PROPOSAL

All the background you collect, from desk research or meetings, informs your relationship with the client. That doesn't mean it'll all get written down or that you'll parrot every fact in meetings – it's just like an iceberg, under the surface, helping you communicate better. Keep up with the background and it becomes stuff you just know, and they'll know you know it.

It may be in the nature of your business to present a written proposal at some point. (You will present in person at a follow-up meeting, rather than by sending the proposal, but at some stage you will leave written material with them.) A good proposal isn't just an offer. It's a signal that says 'I heard, understood, and appreciate, what you said, and here's how I can help.' It creates demand. A good proposal will identify exactly what you've found out from them and what you can do to fulfil their wildest dreams, it is a crisp description of:

- Their present business need
- How you propose to help
- Why your product or service is the best choice

It must include some of the key details the client has given. It must not go on and on about the problem, because that's telling them what they already know. (They probably employ management consultants as it is.) Your focus should be on the solution.

Your proposal doesn't necessarily have to include estimates of price or time, or terms and conditions of sale; these may (depending on the usual process followed by your company) belong in the contract. The proposal will be concise and jargon-free. And most of all, it will differentiate you from the competition.

You will take time to get this right. Who was it that wrote 'Sorry this is such a long letter – I haven't got time to write a short one'?℞ If you hone the document it will take longer. And which would you rather do? Spend time writing eight accurately targeted, winning

---

℞ Blaise Pascal, French mathematician, around 1650. With a quill pen, too.

proposals, or cobble together twenty-eight losers from a template? The proposal must be compelling.

I'm calling the proposal a document, but it may of course be a PowerPoint slideshow or a CAD presentation, a DVD or a one-page letter with samples, specifications, and a price list. Whatever form it takes, it must be concise, informative, compelling.

PowerPoint can be dire, or it can have impact. Keep the backgrounds plain, the words few and bold. Don't crowd the screen with words, bullet points, complex charts. PowerPoint, like other media, is best used as a mere backup to your presentation in person, but you need to get the tone right.

And now for the key to success: *Be there!* Present it yourself. Never, never send a CD-rom or a document attached to an email and expect it to do the presenting for you. Never let anyone in the client company present your solution to the Board, or the Finance Director, or anyone else on your behalf. To do so is to waste all the effort you've put in so far. If for reasons of distance or time a second meeting is impractical, arrange a video-conference. But don't expect a cold proposal to do the work without you.

MAKING WINNING PRESENTATIONS

Let's not be naive! In every audience there will be one person who loathes you on sight. Can't stand your voice, and does not agree with your content. To make matters worse they are usually in the front row glaring at you.

Well, here is a great tip on how to deal with that – *ignore them*!

You cannot win this person over, however well you speak - if you presented an Oscar winning performance with all of the Hollywood panache right in front of them, they'd probably find fault with it.

Yes, it is difficult and unpleasant to feel those negative vibes coming at you but your job is to work with the rest of the audience, who are quite ready to listen. If you focus on Peter Pessimistic you will try too hard, and you will confuse and lose the attention of the rest of your audience!

Remember most audiences want your presentation to go well!

BOMBER B AND THE FOUR E'S

Not the latest band to win 'X Factor', but an easy formula to help you when you start to plan your sales presentation. Just follow this simple structure and think of Bomber B:

B – Bang! *Always start with an attention getting hook or strap-line*

O – Opening *Outline the main messages*

M – Message *Give only 4 - 5 key messages*

B – Bridge *Make a bridge between each key message*

E – Examples *Give examples to help the audience visualise what you mean*

R – Recap *Be sure to summarise what you mean*

B – Bang! *Always finish with a closing 'hook'*

When you start rehearsing your sales presentation, remember the four E's:

E – Energy

E – Enthusiasm

E – Excitement

E – Expertise

THE RULE OF THREE

Aristotle wrote about the rule of three in his book *Rhetoric*. Put simply, people tend to easily remember three things. So, the odds are that people will only remember three things from your presentation!

You can have a huge influence on what they will be! So before you start writing your presentation, plan what your three key messages will be. Once you have these messages, structure the main part of your presentation around your three key messages.

Use the rule of three in other areas of your presentation. Lists of three have been used from early times up to the present day. They are often used by politicians and advertisers who know the value of using the rule of three to sell their ideas.

"Veni, Vidi, Vici" (I came, I saw, I conquered)
JULIUS CAESAR

"Friends, Romans, Countrymen lend me your ears."
WILLIAM SHAKESPEARE

"Location, Location, Location."
THE MANTRA OF EVERY ESTATE AGENT

"Our priorities are Education, Education, Education."
TONY BLAIR

"Stop, look and listen."
PUBLIC SAFETY CAMPAIGN

As your presentation draws to a close your audience must have learned three things about your product or service: its features, advantages and benefits. They won't know these three things because you sat them down and told them, but because you structured your presentation in such a way it made them think about the features, advantages and benefits of your product or service in such a way it created *desire*!

I will delve further into this in the next chapter.

THE PRESENTER'S SECRET TO KEEPING COOL

Have you ever watched someone and simply admired their presentation style? The way they talk with confidence, the way they engage their audience and how they never get flustered. Well, if you have, I would bet anything they all have two things in common. The first is they have all worked very hard on their presentation techniques; after all practice does make perfect. The second is they know the secret I am about to share with you!

It really is quite simple when you think about it; let me start by asking you two questions:

1. Have you ever prepared for a presentation and worried yourself sick that you might forget a critical line?

2. Do you think the presenters you admire never have that concern?

Of course they do! However, they have a contingency plan.

All you need to do is prepare one killer question to ask your audience should you lose your focus. Then relax, because if you do instead of getting into a fluster because you can't remember your next line you simply stop and ask everyone to think about your question.

Not only are you engaging them, you get as much time as you need to re-focus and get back on track.

Before you know it you will be gaining new admirers of your presentation style!

A much better alternative than a bite from that BOA!

 Think of a question for the audience you can memorise. Do it now and capture it. You never know when you might need it!

PRESENTING YOUR PROPOSAL

CHAPTER EIGHT

GAINING AGREEMENT

You've done all the Hard Work – This part is *easy*!

If you've created demand, you are on the home run – but keep your defences at the ready. There may well be obstacles rising up ahead like dragon's teeth.

STILL ON GUARD: PRICE OBJECTIONS

There are nearly always price objections. Buyers, cunning devils as they are, are trained to deflate us; to change the goal-posts at the last minute, or – and this is a favourite – to trim the budget just before you present. They expect this to throw you off balance. If you are unprepared, the Sales-person's Snake will emerge. It's a BOA Constrictor. It squeezes you; you go red, start to panic, and breathe too quickly. You start babbling sentences that begin with *B*asically, *O*bviously, or *A*ctually.

Expect to win the business, but be prepared to lose, so that the BOA Constrictor doesn't get a chance to strangle you.

I admit that I have an advantage in price negotiations in that my business is dedicated to helping my clients make more money. This in itself means I should be seen as a powerful negotiator. But almost any business to business product promises financial improvement of some kind, and there is nothing wrong with negotiating assertively.

I'll give you an example. An MD told me:

"We've spoken to three training providers and we're impressed with all of them. You're the most expensive. You're fifty percent more expensive than the second in line."

"So maybe you should use them," I said "That's if they impress you enough. If ever they don't impress you, come back to me. I won't put my price up. I won't say I told you so. I will be delighted to work with you. The fact is, I have a fundamental problem about promising to make your people better at selling and then saying and by the way I'll drop my price. It's contradictory. Think about it."

"I don't have to," he said "They did drop their price a bit sharpish. You're delivering what they only promised to deliver."

People will ask you for a ten percent reduction. In most industries there is a tactful way to tell the truth, which is: "I would do you no favours by dropping my price because you'd get an inferior service."

What, after all, makes the client suppose that any cut-price service isn't going to cost more in the end? How many times have you seen people make the wrong decision, and wanted to say

"Don't do that; you're wasting your money?" But you can't. You can't ever knock the competition because the customer will internalise a message that standards in your industry are not universally high; and you can't insult the client's own judgement, either.

So guide them towards the correct decision. Let it emerge out of questioning.

Suppose you're selling recruitment services. In recruitment, the best agencies are fussy about the people they sign onto their books. They head-hunt talent, and once they've got good people they make sure that their CV makes them stand out. This takes time: checking-up time, interviewing time, and writing time. None of which comes free.

Of course a company unwilling to spend what recruitment costs can go elsewhere. In fact they could advertise in the broadsheets and weed out the top twenty applications from the four thousand who'll send them an email attachment or fax their résumés or call Human Resources.

And as you can point out to these cheapskates, how would they feel if they tried as hard as that and the recruitment company they should have used had the right person all along, who's now gone to a competitor? And what is the cost to the company of a less-than-perfect candidate?

All well-run businesses are price-sensitive. However, all well-run businesses are willing to spend money on things that matter.

At worst, if you send them a proposal, they open it, flick though and literally look only at the bottom line.

If you're there, you can ask them to identify the key criterion by which they make a decision. Many immediately say:

"Price."

Then you ask:

"It's purely price, then, is it?"

"No, there are other factors of course."

Then you find out what these are, and file them away for future use.

Some people are quite blatant from the start. A man called me and said:

"We're looking for a cheap training course."

I said, "Tell you what – I guarantee you I'll be the cheapest."

"Great!"

"And I guarantee you the course will be garbage, the sales-people will be bored, and your figures will go through the floor."

"Oh," he said. "No, I don't want that."

"You don't want that? You don't want the cheapest course? You've changed your mind then."

In the nicest possible way, you can let these people know that they're talking rubbish. They don't want the cheapest product or service on the market. They want the best. They just find it hard to accept that they will have to pay for it, that's all. Most buyers are trained to push any product or service down to commodity level so they can simply use price as the Dominant Buying Motive. It is rarely the case!

Often "cheap" is confused with "value". Business owners can be sensitive in this regard.

"Why am I looking for a cheap solution? Because it's my money I'm spending. It's my business."

"Oh, so it's your business? And you're looking for a cheap solution?"

"Yes."

"You want it to be successful?"

"Of course I do."

"So what are you going to do when it's successful, go out and buy a Smart Car?"

"No-o…"

"What then?"

"An Aston Martin."

"Why?"

"It is a much better car, it's my dream car."

All the time you're doing this, you are just asking questions.

Your price is part of your brand. If sales-people keep hearing that their product is too expensive, they can start to believe that the price makes it hard to sell. This affects them so that they begin to dread disclosing their price. At worst they mumble and sound apologetic, as if they're half expecting a shocked, negative response.

Remember that fundamentally price is rarely an issue, but the choice of solution to the problem always is. You must believe in the price, which is set for reasons you don't know. What you're selling is a solution. The solution has been worked out over time. It's risen to perfection like a loaf of bread and, like a loaf, if you pay for half, that's what you get.

Let your customer know that you believe the prices are fair.

"Good news!" you'll say "It's only a two and a half percent price increase this year."

"Only!"

"Yes. I thought it was going to be more, when you look at what we do for you…"

Many providers go out of their way to solve customers' problems, and find a year later that the customers have forgotten all about it. You go out of your way to produce accurate material in nine languages in time for Diwali, but when your price rises a gnat's knee above inflation, everybody's moaning. Be proud to quote your price.

You may be selling something intangible, like design or branding. If someone is shocked by the price of creative work, it's usually because they don't understand how many hours of work it takes and how much imagination and skill goes into doing it. However, they will find out how reasonable the fee is when you offer to charge them at your hourly rate.

As a last resort – let's say your potential client has stuck. If this person were in a romantic novel, you'd call him commitment-phobic. He's heard the arguments and is chewing his lip.

Okay. It's time to leave.

There used to be a TV series called Colombo. Peter Falk played a slight, hunched, self-effacing cop who always wore (in Beverly Hills, in summer) a grubby raincoat that billowed round him like a tent. This guy never made an entrance. Instead he sidled into the scene of the crime, muttered a few apologetic questions, agreed with everybody and then headed for the door. (Cutaway to relieved look between victim's husband and glamorous au pair.)

With his hand touching the handle, he'd pause. Finger to his nose, thoughtfully. Turn; and snap his fingers.

"You know what puzzles me? When Mr Delmar found the body ... how come Mamie Delmar was still in the bath?"

The single flaw in the defence! Victim's husband crumples.

Okay. Back in Peterborough, it's time to accept defeat.

"I know – I'm afraid the price concerns you. You know I respect your decision."

You fold your laptop; you slip it into its case.

The prospect, frown clearing, gets up.

You get to your feet too, and take a step towards the door.

Prospect reaches for door-handle...

And you come out with your one killer question:

"But let me ask you this. Is the price of ownership more significant than the cost to the business of not having it?"

Breathtaking.

Now get it in writing!

THE TIPPING POINT

Some sales trainers say *all* objections are positive, because they provide an opportunity to overcome them. That's positive thinking for you. According to this rule, getting measles is great, because your immune system learns how to cope. If you really thought objections were an opportunity, you would talk yourself out of sales by dreaming them up.

Draw two intersecting lines at right angles. The horizontal axis measures time, and the vertical one measures interest. Isn't it usual, when we start talking to a new customer, that because we've spent no time there is no interest? But as we spend time, and objections are dealt with, interest starts to climb.

So when you are expert in using the ABCD of selling, you will reach a point where interest has largely overcome objections. That is the tipping point. Any objections before are negative; beyond that point, they are positive; beyond that, they eventually reach another tipping point, which is negative and often final.

Malcolm Gladwell has written a best-seller about this.☞ There are tipping points in the spread of disease (when it becomes an epidemic and when it dies out naturally), the status of a handbag (when it shifts from cult item to fashionista's must-have to high-street cliché), and in the rise and fall of crime waves, bestsellers, teenage smoking, and everything else from ageing to yawning.

There are three characteristics of anything that has a tipping point: one, it's contagious; two, little causes can have big effects; and three, the tipping point isn't gradual – it's sudden. And when you are selling to a group of people, or trying to change their opinion in any way, you will recognise that this happens. There comes a moment when the views of the crowd swing one way: your way. They're all nodding, they're all creating a mental picture and replaying to themselves everything they've just learned, and you know you've got them. From then on, they're imagining life with the

---

☞ *The Tipping Point,* Abacus, 2000.

product or service, and implicitly asking you how they'll deal with snags. These are positive objections.

COMMITMENT

If you've had to overcome objections and your client has moved from a 'maybe' to a 'yes', pin it down now.

If you don't, in their minds it's a great idea but not yet signed off. Either they'll start looking at competitors in your field that they'd always dismissed until you convinced them they needed the service, or – which is even more likely – the original objection will resurface. When you get back to the office and call them, it's:

"I've been thinking…"

And you're not in front of them now. The tipping point has been passed, and you won't pass it twice.

Your opportunity to sign them up is when you have successfully presented. If this is a large organisation and you haven't yet asked about their buying process, this is the moment to do so.

"I suppose at this stage we need to raise a purchase order?"

"Because, if you need this for the exhibition, and that's on the 15th of April, we'd better not lose any time. We don't want everything happening in a rush at the last minute."

You sound professional; you're working backwards from their deadlines to make it clear that you've got their interests at heart. Use their targets.

Don't forget that you can use targets with the gatekeeper too.

"Corporate Affairs please."

"What's it about?"

"They know me."

"I'm afraid I'm under instruction to ask what it's concerning."

"You've got an exhibition on the 15th of April which we're working on with them, and if I don't talk to them today I won't be able to complete the plans for your exhibition stand."

"Oh! All right." You're put through!

FAB STORIES: FEATURES, ADVANTAGES & BENEFITS

Before I go any further I would like you to think for a moment about these three well used words. When you have done that, write down your understanding of each one in a sales context.

- A Feature is ...
- An Advantage is ...
- A Benefit is ...

When you have done that, think of any product or service that comes to mind, then list:

- One Feature
- One Advantage
- One Benefit

Do you notice anything different about the relationship between the three?

- A Feature is a statement about the product.
- An Advantage is the consequence of the feature.
- A Benefit is what impact it has on the *individual* customer.

It is imperative to understand that the first two are constant; however the 'Benefit' is *not*!

I get frustrated with marketing departments who spend a lot of money on marketing collateral without realising this important fact. They assume the benefits to customers are always the same and print them on their product sheets. They should in fact label them as "Potential Benefits": it is the sales-person's mission to establish what will benefit the customer and sell it accordingly!

There has been a lot of talk over the years about the divide between sales and marketing; this book is not going to add any fuel to that fire, as I am equally frustrated with sales-people who fail to realise one simple but critical factor.

What benefits one customer may not benefit another!

I remember accompanying a sales-person once who was busy telling his potential customer about the features and advantages of this particular machine. He made the claim:

"And the real benefit to you is you can run this with one less person, saving you a whole salary and improving the return on investment."

The customer replied:

"That's fantastic! Who shall I fire? My father or my brother?"

As a small family business the potential benefit did not appeal to that individual customer.

Remember – it is your job to establish what will benefit your customer! How else can you create demand?

THE CLOSE

We must know when to be humble and when to be assertive. The close is the time to be assertive.

If you don't close assertively, you are demonstrating that you are unsure of your proposal – that you don't know it will do what you say it will do. And if your message is 'I'm not convinced that this is any good but I still want you to buy it' do you think your audience is disillusioned? This is why people think we are sharks.

When I say 'be confident', I'm too polite: say what you mean and then *shut up*.

Use the power of silence.

Have you heard the phrase 'he talked himself out of the sale'? If you bang on and on, you'll miss the tipping point, the buying signal. You'll be so busy pitching that the opportunity to close the deal will pass you by.

A great many sales-people feel that closing is their weakest skill. If they are working with the old-fashioned model of selling – Always Be Closing – they're probably right. They've hammered the buyer into submission and by the time they get to the final run, they're both exhausted.

There used to be a three-day training course: 'One Hundred Ways to Close a Deal.' Have you ever met anyone who could remember a hundred ways to close? And do you believe that thirty of the ways weren't variations on a theme? And how many sales-people must have been terrified – 'But I'm not a tactician! Which one should I use?' Or 'I could've got the business but I didn't know which close to go with…'

Selling requires lightning-fast, intuitive responses to the reactions you're getting from buyers. If, at the tipping point itself, you throw up a left-brain problem like 'which of these hundred doors do I go through?' most salesmen will gasp like stranded fish.

So learning a hundred ways to close a deal is inappropriate; it's an unsophisticated approach.

Everything in the ABCD of selling is hinged around creating demand. We shouldn't need to close in any mechanistic way if we've done things right from the start. We will be dealing with people who will want to buy from us, if we've done our job properly. So all we need to learn are six possible routes to finalising the transaction. You won't have to panic about which one to use; they'll become intuitive choices, like changing gear when you're driving a car.

The six ways are:

1. the trial close
2. the minor decision close
3. the direct decision close
4. the assumptive close
5. the alternative choice close
6. the benefits close

TRIAL CLOSE

You are testing the water.

"Would you like me to organise a trial run?"

With any close, your defence must be prepared. They may say "No."

The stock response is:

"You must have a good reason for saying that. Would you mind telling me what it is?"

"Umm – I'm not sure."

"If you were sure what would you say?"

Always remember how to get into your *Zenith Zone*, and your armoury of stock phrases. Don't panic: maintain your focus.

MINOR DECISION CLOSE

This is similar to the trial close but gives you an opportunity to show commitment. You might say:

"I tell you what, shall we go ahead and get the cabling/pilot study/outline drawings done?"

You're proposing to make a start on the work, and if they are going to spend money on that, they will probably commit themselves in due course to the whole job. So you're asking them to take a minor decision because you can see that a big one is just too much to handle all at once.

This works well. However it should not be confused with 'let us have a free sample of your work/free trial of your services' which is a favourite in buyer's markets such as television; offering to work for nothing is rarely a foot in the door and never, ever a close.

DIRECT DECISION CLOSE

"Given what we've said, are you happy to proceed?" This is a closed question that prompts a "Yes. I always nod my head while I'm asking this."

As for when to ask – if you're in your *Zenith Zone* you will be alert, and will subliminally notice the tipping point. If you're sure this is the moment, ask the closed question and keep quiet.

If they hesitate or mutter among themselves, say nothing. Use the power of silence.

If they ask a question, reply briefly. Don't start to oversell.

And be prepared, with stock phrases and a positive face, for a negative response.

ASSUMPTIVE CLOSE

This has become a cliché. For years, the foot soldiers of the sales world would prop themselves up against a shop counter with an order form on a clipboard.

"Right. Is it one T in Patel? Let's see. Mars Bars – how many do you want?"

Some businesses, in particular - when I last looked – conservatory manufacturers, still train their sales force to put down details on paper during the course of a sale - a strategy designed to lead to an assumptive close. Elsewhere, this close is going out of favour because if it's used unsubtly customers can feel frog-marched into buying. And as we know, that's the worst possible outcome because it makes them feel bad about themselves – they seethe under the surface with unfocussed bitterness and anger, because they weren't assertive enough to put their foot down.

Another reason for its decline is practical. There are fewer chances to sell at transactional level these days.

Besides, what does the sales-person say if the customer snaps:

"Hold on. You're assuming rather a lot, aren't you? When did you hear me say I wanted Mars Bars?"

If you ever try an assumptive close and this happens, be prepared to reverse out smoothly and without panic with your hands in the air.

"I'm certainly not assuming. The way I work is to get everything onto a worthless piece of paper. It's a worthless piece of paper as long as it doesn't have your signature on the back of it. It's not an order form until it does. I'll be leaving it with you and you can make up your own mind, and if you want to rip it up you can."

ALTERNATIVE CHOICE CLOSE

If they have a choice of two, they'll pick one. Whichever it is they're placing an order with you. Half now and the rest later, or the whole delivery at once? Before Easter or after? With our branding or yours? This is a less problematic, more effective version of the assumptive close.

BENEFITS CLOSE

This is also known as the pencil sell. You briefly reprise, point by point, the benefits of the product or service. If it's business to business there will be a financial reward or saving involved.

"We discussed [benefit], and it would save you ..." and you list everything. You continue:

"So what you are really saying is – we're offering you the opportunity to save four million, but you've got to spend two hundred thousand to do it."

Put that way, it's a no-brainer. When you've got that sort of power in your proposal, use it that way. Let people know. Since about 1980, the benefits close has changed the world. "You'll buy our computer system for 400K and by the end of the year you'll save five million in labour."

Now shut up!

They look at each other; they all start nodding.

"That's a yes then? How many do you want? Two or four?"

 Now think of your business world and consider how you could use the closing techniques outlined above.

Remember: The difference between mediocre and successful sales-people is that successful sales-people make things happen. Now go out and change the world!

GAINING AGREEMENT

CHAPTER NINE

POSITIVE REPETITION

I was taught in my time in corporate life that "knowledge is power". I used to believe it, but I was wrong. Knowledge is nothing *unless you use that knowledge*!

One important piece of knowledge you need to remember and use is that you are only as good as your last set of results!

You can end the year thirty percent above plan, but next year the pressure is on once again. That's the way it is in the sales environment, so once you have the order enjoy the thrill momentarily, then get on with your job. It never stops!

The point is I have met many sales-people who know this and they all understand why it is the case, but only a small percentage of them *adhere* to it! If you are one of the masses of sales-people who think "this is it, I have found my true vocation in life" please ask yourself this one question, "Can I do this job well for as long as I want to?"

REMEMBERING AIDA

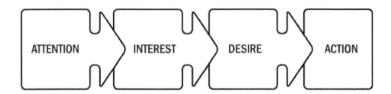

In 1898, the American advertising and sales pioneer, E. St. Elmo Lewis developed a practical sales tool using his observations of sales-people and his management insight. He created his AIDA funnel model on customer studies in the US life insurance market to explain the mechanisms of personal selling. Lewis stated that the most successful sales-people followed a hierarchical, four-layer process using the four cognitive phases that buyers follow when accepting a new idea or purchasing a new product.

The AIDA model describes the basic process by which people become motivated to act on a purchase and is based on external stimuli from sales representatives. This motivation to make a purchase depends on:

1) *Attention* of the existence of a product or service.

2) *Interest* in paying attention to how the product benefits them.

3) *Desire* for the product.

3) *Action* – the natural result of moving through the first three stages!

This basic sales model has served us well for over 100 years and is still seen as in integral part of the sales process in many large organisations to this day.

Can you think of some good reasons why this model has lasted the test of time?

I think one of the primary reasons is that it is focused around the customer! So many sales process models are designed around the sales-person or the organisational needs and not the client. So the key then is *how*?

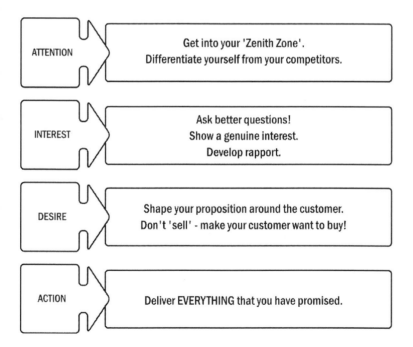

ATTENTION	Get into your 'Zenith Zone'. Differentiate yourself from your competitors.
INTEREST	Ask better questions! Show a genuine interest. Develop rapport.
DESIRE	Shape your proposition around the customer. Don't 'sell' - make your customer want to buy!
ACTION	Deliver EVERYTHING that you have promised.

MAKING TACTICAL CHANGES

If you constantly work with the right attitude, it gets easier to adapt to a situation in order to give you the best chance of success.

I was with Kris Akabusi a few years ago, and he related an incident that had happened the night before the 1991 Great Britain relay team were going to run in the final of the World championships in Tokyo. That night, their coach had asked them if they were going to be happy with a silver medal?

They looked at each other in horror. If he didn't think they were good enough, he'd left it a bit late to say so!

"No-o. What are you saying?"

"I'm saying," said the coach "If we run the race the way we have run previous races you will not win gold!" the other team members (Derek Redmond, John Regis and Roger Black) looked at him in disbelief:

"Are you saying we are not good enough?" they asked.

There was silence.

"I think it's time to do something different," the coach said.

It is well known that a relay race it is the fastest runner who runs last and sprints to the finish. But their coach's advice, with just twelve hours to go before the big race, they defied convention. They would put their fastest runner first.

The rival teams saw the new line-up and momentarily lost focus. Was the fastest guy starting the race because he was way off form? Or was the fourth man suddenly performing amazingly well? Concentration was shot to pieces. Their main rivals (The USA) were not in their *Zenith Zone*, they were confused, But Akabusi, and his team mates Roger Black, John Regis, and Derek Redmond most certainly were.

The USA were the better team yet a bold, decisive, last-minute tactical change ensured the British team won gold.

I have seen too many sales-people set about their challenges without thinking of how they are going to achieve their goals. This means their strategy is based on one thing: *hope*.

Let me tell you now: hope is not a strategy. By doing something different you can change results. Back in 1991, the only difference between failure and excellence was that team's ability to make a decision and be totally committed it. There was no time to waste on doubt.

So remember to stay in your *Zenith Zone*; because nobody ever took a big step forward without making changes, and you need to handle change positively.

POSITIVE REPETITION

CHAPTER TEN

IMPLEMENTATION & RETENTION

ENSURE A SMOOTH CUSTOMER EXPERIENCE. MANAGING THE 'CUSTOMER SATISFACTION GAP'

So you've won the business. Well Done. Now comes another challenge: keep it. This is not always as easy as it sounds.

Have a look at the image below. It shows why there is such a strong chance of losing business before you gain a trading relationship.

When you initially qualify a potential customer your commitment is normally high (if this isn't the case, stop here and go back a few chapters!). You are likely to be more enthused than your potential customer is at this time. Then as you progress the sale both of you become more committed to the initiative. You then reach a very important point. The Point of Sale. The day you get the order. This is when it all changes. You have done your job; all you have to do is get your order on the system and then get on with winning more business - after all you have got targets to hit haven't you? But what about your customer? No longer a potential, now a client. What about their expectations? Yes, they have gone up as they have just committed to spend some money with you.

This is where the 'Customer Satisfaction Gap' is formed.

It is acceptable for this to happen, with one caveat:

Your company has to understand exactly what the customer expects and delegate that responsibility to someone!

In other words, if you are going to be heading off to find more new business, someone has to ensure the customer's expectations are met. If this fails to happen you will lose the customer faster than you gained them. So you need to work to eliminate this gap by ensuring that the customer is constantly receiving the level of service and support that meets or exceeds their expectations.

Make sure the business fully understands what has to be done to create the right first impression, and make sure somebody has the responsibility to deliver it!

CRM systems are ideally placed to help solve this issue.

WHAT CRM REALLY STANDS FOR

Most sales-people today have some sort of CRM system to complete, and I know a lot who are not happy about this, as they think it can be a waste of their time. I often ask these people what CRM stands for, so I will ask you the same question.

What does CRM stand for?

I guess you have written 'Customer Relationship Management', and of course you would be right. However I think there is another acronym we can use here which symbolises the importance of a CRM system. Any ideas?

Turn the page and I will tell you.

C - Can't
R - Remember
M - Much

Too many people rely on their memory in their quest to provide customer satisfaction: this is a recipe for disaster! Have you ever heard the saying that 'The success of your business depends on the way you treat your customers'? This is one of the most important truths of business. But how can you ensure you treat your customers in the right way when each customer has different likes, dislikes and behavioural patterns? Well, relying on your memory certainly isn't the best strategy. I know many sales-people who find this element of their job mundane and boring, but how can we expect the organisation to manage the 'Customer Satisfaction Gap' if we don't provide the information that will tell them what has to be done? Even with years of accumulated knowledge, there's always room for improvement. Customer needs change over time, and technology can make it easier to track those changes and ensure that everyone in an organisation can exploit this information.

DELIVER EVERYTHING YOU PROMISE!

"A promise made is a debt unpaid."
ROBERT SERVICE

I am sure you have heard people say that sales-people should under-promise and over-deliver. Well, I am not sure that this is the most appropriate strategy in today's competitive business world. Think about it: if you under-promise you might not get the chance to over-deliver because you may not win the business in the first place. I will concede that it's better to 'under-promise and over-deliver' than not deliver what you promised. The most important message to convey is that the customer must get what you have promised.

Set realistic timelines and budgets and add a safety margin so you can deliver on time what you promised. You can't control everything, but you can be on top of everything that happens along the way. You don't want that to mess up your first sale with your new customer, yet Murphy's Law says you will. (Remember Murphy's Law? If it can go wrong it *will* go wrong!) Well, in relation to first time deliveries, I personally think Murphy was an optimist!

There is a good reason for this. You have no trading history, nothing to refer back to, no experience within the organisation to ensure a smooth transaction. So it's down to you to make certain your promises become reality. After all, you customer gave the order to you, so it has to be down to you to deliver every aspect of the proposition that created that desire to place the order with you.

IMPLEMENTATION & RETENTION

AND FINALLY

I hope you have enjoyed reading this book, and more importantly I hope the content will help you to improve your strategies. Selling is a wonderful profession whether you work in America or any other part of the world; however it isn't an easy job. A lot of people fail to reach their full potential because they believe they can achieve all of their expectations without too much difficulty, and some even believe they know everything they need to know about selling. Thankfully you don't (or you probably wouldn't have bought this book!). In selling, like most professions, you will never know everything; my advice to anyone who honestly believes they do is to start looking for a new job as you will soon start to become complacent and that will reflect in your results. Remember what I told you earlier: you are only as good as your last set of results!

So to help you continue to grow and develop in your sales career I would like to leave you with my A to Z of selling:

A   *Attitude*
B   *Benefits*
C   *Commitment*
D   *Desire*

E	*Enthusiasm*
F	*Focus*
G	*Grow*
H	*Help customers find the best solutions for them*
I	*Influence*
J	*Justify your price*
K	*Keep Control*
L	*Listen*
M	*Motivation*
N	*Network*
O	*Opportunities*
P	*Passion*
Q	*Questions*
R	*Relationships*
S	*Solutions*
T	*Telling Isn't Selling*
U	*Understand*
V	*Value*
W	*Who / Why / What / When / Where*
X	*Xcellence (I know but can you think of a better one? You did get five Ws)*
Y	*You Factor*
Z	*Zenith Zone*

Why don't you create your own A to Z? You can even send it to me and I may feature it on our website.

I wish you every success in your career, and by the way I believe success is the maximum utilisation of the skills and ability you have!

BIBLIOGRAPHY

MY TOP 20 RECOMMENDATIONS

1. *Persuasion*, James Borg, ISBN 9780273712992
2. *Secrets of Question-based Selling*, Thomas Freese , ISBN 157015882
3. *Spin Selling*, Neil Rackham, ISBN 0070511136
4. *The New Solution Selling*, Keith M. Eades, ISBN 0071435395
5. *Selling the Invisible*, Harry Beckwith, ISBN 1587990660
6. *The Sales Bible*, Jeffrey Gitomer, ISBN 0471456292
7. *Sales Dogs*, Blair Singer, ISBN 0446678333
8. *Tough Calls*, Josh Gordon, ISBN 0814479251
9. *Consultative Closing*, Greg Bennet, ISBN 978814473993
10. *Selling Is Dead*, Miller Sinkovitz, ISBN 0471721115
11. *The Prime Solution*, Jeff Thull, ISBN 0793195225
12. *Customer Concentric Selling*, Bosworth Holland, ISBN 0071425454
13. *Hope is Not a Strategy*, Rick Page, ISBN 0071418717
14. *Rethinking The Sales Force*, Rackham, DeVincentis, ISBN 0071342532
15. *Why People Don't Buy Things*, Washburn Wallace, ISBN 0738200123
16. *The Art of Talking So People Listen*, Paul W. Swets, ISBN 0130478377
17. *Strategic Selling*, Miller Heimana Tuleja, ISBN 1850919518
18. *Selling Results*, Bill Stinnett, ISBN 007147787X
19. *Mastering the Complex Sale*, Jeff Thull, ISBN 0471431
20. *Stop Telling, Start Selling*, Linda Richardson, ISBN 0070525587

Also Available from Bookshaker.com

"*Beginners and experts alike will find this book filled with useful information. I wish I had had a book like this when I was learning NLP!*"

Romilia Ready, Lead Author,
NLP for Dummies® & NLP Workbook for Dummies®

Persuasion Skills
BLACK BOOK

Practical NLP Language Patterns for Getting The Response You Want

Rintu Basu

FREE INSIDE
'Black Book'
Persuasion
Training
E-course

Act Your Way To Sales Success

SELL YOUR SELF!

BRYAN McCORMACK

Foreword by RINTU BASU author of 'Persuasion Skills Black Book'